Instructor's Notes

Everything's an Argument with Readings

Fifth Edition

Andrea A. Lunsford
John J. Ruszkiewicz
Keith Walters

Prepared by John Kinkade, Jodi Egerton, and Taryne Hallett

Bedford/St. Martin's
Boston ◆ New York

Manufactured in the United States of America.

4 3 2 1 0 9
f e d c b a

For information, write: Bedford/St. Martin's, 75 Arlington Street, Boston, MA 02116 (617-399-4000)

ISBN-10: 0-312-60024-0
ISBN-13: 978-0-312-60024-2

Contents

Introduction ix

1. Everything Is an Argument 1
2. Arguments Based on Emotion: Pathos 7
3. Arguments Based on Character: Ethos 10
4. Arguments Based on Facts and Reason: Logos 14
5. Rhetorical Analysis 17
6. Academic Arguments 20
7. Structuring Arguments 23
8. Arguments of Fact 27
9. Arguments of Definition 30
10. Evaluations 34
11. Causal Arguments 37
12. Proposals 39
13. Style in Arguments 41
14. Visual Arguments 44
15. Presenting Arguments 46
16. What Counts as Evidence 48
17. Fallacies of Argument 51
18. Intellectual Property, Academic Integrity, and Avoiding Plagiarism 53
19. Evaluating and Using Sources 55
20. Documenting Sources 57

Chapter 21: How Does Popular Culture Stereotype *You*? 59

Sam Dillon, *Evictions at Sorority Raise Issue of Bias* 59

Ellen Goodman, *The Culture of Thin Bites Fiji* 61

Anne E. Becker, *Abstract, Discussion, and Conclusions of Television, Disordered Eating, and Young Women in Fiji: Negotiating Body Image and Identity during Rapid Social Change* 63

Making a Visual Argument

KennethCole.com, *We All Walk in Different Shoes* 65

Barbara Munson, *Common Themes and Questions about the Use of "Indian" Logos* 66

Joe Lapointe, *Bonding over a Mascot* 69

Stuart Elliott, *Uncle Ben, Board Chairman* 71

Charles A. Riley II, *Disability and the Media: Prescriptions for Change* 72

Chapter 22: How Many Friends Have You Made Today? 75

danah m. boyd and Nicole B. Ellison, *Social Network Sites: Definition, History, and Scholarship* 75

Office of the Privacy Commissioner of Canada, *A Friend of a Friend of a Friend Knows You're on Vacation* 77

Heather Havenstein, *One in Five Employers Uses Social Networks in Hiring Process* 79

Tamar Lewin, *Study Finds Teenagers' Internet Socializing Isn't Such a Bad Thing* 81

Mizuko Ito et al., *"Executive Summary," Living and Learning with New Media* 82

Mizuko Ito et al., *Geeking Out* 84

Neal Conan, Kim Zetter, Andy Carvin, and Callers, *Is Creating a Fake Online Profile a Criminal Act?* 85

Charles M. Blow, *A Profile of Online Profiles* 87

Chapter 23: What's It Like to Be Bilingual in the United States? 90

Rochelle Sharpe, *English Loses Ground* 90

Hyon B. Shin with Rosalind Bruno, *Language Use and English-Speaking Ability: 2000* 93

Sandra Cisneros, *From "Bien Pretty"* 95

Marjorie Agosín, *Always Living in Spanish* 96

Marjorie Agosín, *English* 96

Firoozeh Dumas, *The "F Word"* 97

Lan Cao, *The Gift of Language* 99

Amy Tan, *Mother Tongue* 100

Making a Visual Argument: Public Service Announcements in Spanish

National Institute of Mental Health, *En la comunidad latina tenemos una cultura de silencio* 102

Agency for Healthcare Research and Quality, *Non eres un superheroe* 102

Amy Martinez Starke, *Hmong Elder Didn't Forget the Old Ways* 103

Chapter 24: Why Worry about Food and Water? 106

Mark Bittman, *Why Take Food Seriously?* 106

Wynne Wright and Gerad Middendorf, *Introduction: Fighting Over Food—Change in the Agrifood System* 108

Solomon H. Katz, *The World Food Crisis: An Overview of the Causes and Consequences* 110

Kathy Freston, *Vegetarian Is the New Prius* 112

Making a Visual Argument

Claire Ironside, *Apples to Oranges* 114

Wikipedia, *Local Food* 116

Mark Coleman, Review of *Bottlemania: How Water Went on Sale and Why We Bought It* 118

Elizabeth Royte, Excerpt from *Bottlemania: How Water Went on Sale and Why We Bought It* 119

Cook's Country Magazine, Ready-to-Bake Chocolate Chip Cookies and *Cook's Illustrated Magazine, Solving the Mystery of the Chewy Chocolate Chip Cookie* 121

Chapter 25: What Role Should Religion Play in Public Life? 124

Pew Global Attitudes Project, *When It Comes to Religion, the United States Is an Outlier* 125

Laurie Goodstein, *More Religion, but Not the Old-Time Kind* 126

D. Michael Lindsay, *Evangelicalism Rebounds in Academe* 128

Michelle Bryant, *Selling Safe Sex in Public Schools* 131
Melanie Springer Mock, *Separation of Church and State: A War on Christmas and Other Misguided Notions* 133
Antonin Scalia, *God's Justice and Ours* 135
Mariam Rahmani, *Wearing a Head Scarf Is My Choice as a Muslim: Please Respect It* 137
Randy Cohen, *Between the Sexes* 138
This I Believe
Albert Einstein, *An Ideal of Service to Our Fellow Man* 139
Eboo Patel, *We Are Each Other's Business* 139
Penn Jillette, *There Is No God* 139

Chapter 26: What Should "Diversity on Campus" Mean? 143
Making a Visual Argument: Student-Designed Diversity Posters
Joseph Wagner , *Peeling Off Labels* 143
Stephanie Heyman, *Everyone a Part, No One Apart* 143
Melanie Frost, *Embracing Diversity in University Residences* 144
Hannah Leimback, *Identities Are Infinite . . . What's Yours?* 144
Megan Stampfli, *Embrace Diversity* 144
Sarah Karnasiewicz, *The Campus Crusade for Guys* 145
Making a Visual Argument: Cartoonists Take on Affirmative Action
Mike Lester, *It's GOT to Be the Shoes* 147
Dennis Draughon, *Supreme Irony* 147
Mike Thompson, *Daniel Lives on Detroit's Eastside . . .* 147
Signe Wilkinson, *Admissions* 147
Dean Camp, *Pricey* 147
David Horowitz, *In Defense of Intellectual Diversity* 149
Stanley Fish, *"Intellectual Diversity": The Trojan Horse of a Dark Design* 151

Patricia Cohen, *Professors' Liberalism Contagious? Maybe Not* 153

Mack D. Mariani and Gordon J. Hewitt, *Indoctrination U.? Faculty Ideology and Changes in Student Political Orientation* (Excerpt) 155

Libby Sander, *Blue-Collar Boomers Take Work Ethic to College* 158

Edward F. Palm, *The Veterans Are Coming! The Veterans Are Coming!* 160

Walter Benn Michaels, *The Trouble with Diversity: How We Learned to Love Identity and Ignore Inequality* 162

Chapter 27: What Are You Working For? 166

Dave Isay, ed., *Dr. Monica Mayer, 45, Interviewed by Her Cousin and Patient, Spencer Wilkinson, Jr., 39; Ken Kobus, 58, Tells His Friend Ron Baraff, 42, about Making Steel* 166

Lisa W. Foderaro, *The Well-to-Do Get Less So, and Teenagers Feel the Crunch* 168

Charles Murray, *Should the Obama Generation Drop Out?* 170

Letters to the Editor, *Should a College Degree Be Essential?* 170

U.S. Bureau of Labor Statistics, *Education Pays* 172

Laurence Shatkin, *Education Pays, but Perhaps Less Than You Thought* 172

Sandy Baum and Jennifer Ma for the College Board, *Education Pays: The Benefits of Higher Education for Individuals and Society* 174

Alesia Montgomery, *Kitchen Conferences and Garage Cubicles: The Merger of Home and Work in the 24–7 Global Economy* 175

Stewart D. Friedman, *The Fallacy of "Work-Life Balance"* and *Take the Four-Way View* 177

Introduction

The title of this text—*Everything's an Argument*—is more than just a snappy phrase. It represents our conviction that all language, whether written or spoken, visual or textual, is *motivated.* Because language is a human activity and because humans exist in a complex world of goals, purposes, and activities, language cannot be anything *but* motivated. In the words of Kenneth Burke, whose work has been central to the conception of this text, language is a form of "symbolic action": it gets things done in the world, acting on people and situations. The weak version of this argument claims simply that language has effects in the world or that people use language to accomplish ends; most of us would have no difficulty accepting that proposition.

But we hold to the strong version of the argument, maintaining, with Burke, that all language is *inherently* a form of argument. In this formulation of the claim, people use language to create *identification* between themselves and their audience. We cannot escape this naturally human function of language. The flip side of the argument that all language is motivated is powerful, too: all language is open to interpretation and negotiation. Production and analysis of language in this model require not just reason but also all the sensory faculties and an awareness of the rhetor's and the audience's history and experiences. Burke's definition of language's scope and power makes apparently simple activities—chatting with friends, reading the newspaper, writing a note to yourself—into scenes of argument and identification. We are all "wordlings," made of language as much as users of it.

In *A Grammar of Motives*, Burke introduced the dramatistic pentad, a way of describing the human uses of language and the relationships among people, their language, and their world. The five elements—act, scene, agent, agency, purpose—do not appear explicitly in this text, but the concepts remain important to us. The text's focus on the ethical problems of language use reflects our sense that responsible argument always considers the rhetorical situation in all its fullness; without attention to the ethical positions writers and readers inhabit, rhetoric—productive *and* analytic—is irresponsible. We hope that this text will help students learn to use language well, as readers and as writers, and that students will come to understand the complex role language plays in their life and world.

Notes for Using the Readings

You've already noticed that the anthology of readings in *Everything's an Argument with Readings* (Chapters 21–27) is quite different from the collections of readings in other rhetoric texts. Consistent with the title of the book, the readings include traditional essays as well as arguments in other genres—newspaper articles, poems, cartoons, Web sites, and more. Some genres may be unfamiliar at first, but we hope you will discover, as we have, that the variety gives you a great deal of flexibility and allows you to approach argumentation from fresh perspectives that can help your students readily grasp the value of rhetoric in real-life applications.

Each chapter's readings contain at least one traditional essay that can serve as a model of the kind of writing that students are learning to produce. News pieces can be especially valuable for helping students learn to identify authors' points of view, even in contexts where the writer's stance isn't overtly stated. In the Respond exercises following each reading, students may be asked to find and state the positions taken in the journalistic pieces, or they may be asked to redraft an argument into academic essay format. Such exercises have a threefold purpose—to test comprehension, to assist students in understanding the importance of style and tone in various genres, and to give students practice in crafting academic prose. An additional value of these exercises is that they incorporate ideas and conclusions already provided by the reading, thereby enabling students to focus strictly on the craft of writing.

The chapter topics were chosen for their currency in public discourse and for their complexity. None of them can be considered a simple pro/con question or a clear-cut issue of conventional conservative/liberal opposition. We expect one of the benefits of this variety to be that the alliances among students in your classroom discussions throughout the term will shift with the various topics, allowing students to both acquaint themselves with a broader range of ideas and find commonality with a broader range of people than they might otherwise. The readings within each chapter contribute to that complexity both by their content and by the variety of genres and media represented.

The exercises following the readings are quite varied, although there is at least one writing assignment for nearly every reading. Many questions require students to synthesize information from other readings in the same chapter. Most of the questions, except where stated otherwise, are intended for individual responses. In addition, many of them can provide focus for classroom discussion or small-group work.

The Structure of the *Instructor's Notes*

The text of these notes is arranged to follow the main text chapter by chapter. For the rhetoric chapters (1–20), the notes for each chapter outline some of the problems you might face while teaching it, suggest some solutions, and address the chapter exercises, with ideas for extending those exercises beyond the text. The exercises are open-ended, so our notes are, too: there are no easy answers to any of the problems we suggest in each chapter. (Please note that a few exercises, those which might elicit especially varied responses, are not addressed in these notes.) Also included are suggestions for using the Not Just Words activity in each chapter that focuses on visual argument.

For each of the seven chapters of readings (21–27), the corresponding chapter of the *Notes* begins with an introduction to the issues addressed in the chapter, along with some general questions that the issues raise. Then we provide possible answers for the Respond exercises at the end of each reading. Most questions in these exercises are quite open-ended, and the answers will vary; in many cases we've suggested one or more possibilities. No attempt has been made to provide answers for writing assignments. At the end of each chapter are wrap-up exercises that incorporate material from two or more readings; some of these questions would be suitable for in-class essay writing.

We also provide a suggested classroom exercise for each reading. The concept behind the classroom exercises is to give each reading a session's worth (about an hour) of class time, although you may be budgeting class time very differently. Except where otherwise noted, the exercises are discussion questions based on the reading. Some of the classroom exercises focus on the content of the reading, some require students to think about the worlds they know in terms of the arguments presented in the reading, and some ask students to analyze the reading in terms of specific rhetorical techniques or lines of argument. In most cases, students should have done the reading already and perhaps answered one or more of the questions that follow it. With some modification, however, many of the questions could work well as prereading exercises to get students thinking about a topic or to explore their preconceptions. If your class is small, everyone can participate in a single discussion. You may, however, wish to break the class into small groups to maximize the speaking opportunities for every student. Be sure to save some time at the end of the session for groups to summarize their discussion for the whole class (this is great practice in summarizing and constructing oral arguments).

If your class periods are sufficiently long, give groups 10 or 15 minutes to prepare a discussion, and select one group to present its arguments and ideas to the class (for 5 or 10 minutes). As an additional reinforcement, the other students can analyze and discuss the rhetorical techniques used in the group's presentation. If you retain the same groups over several discussion sessions, each group could have a turn at presenting its arguments to the entire class.

CHAPTER 1

Everything Is an Argument

Everything's an Argument presents an extended argument for the idea that all language is a form of motivated action, an idea that may not make sense to many first-year students. Even confident and experienced writers will find new ideas in this chapter, and for many students these unfamiliar ideas may make for something of a conceptual mess. Give yourself and the students a few weeks to use the terminology, practice analyzing texts, and ask questions.

The most important lesson in this chapter is that all language and even images can serve as argument. Some first-year students have difficulty understanding *argument* as anything but "disagreement," and getting them to accept the word as meaning "making a point" or "reasoned inquiry" can take some time. Students may also have some difficulty making the distinction between *argument* and *persuasion*. As an in-class activity, you might ask your students to write a one-sentence definition of one of the terms. Then have students read their definitions aloud without identifying the term. The rest of the class can try to guess which word is being defined and explain their guesses.

A second important lesson in this chapter is that rhetorical situations vary widely, ranging from the obviously persuasive (Malcolm Gladwell's attack on American health care) to the poetic (Michael Lassell's poem about a brother's death). Understanding how arguments change depending on contexts and even understanding the contexts themselves can be challenging for students. Fortunately, even seemingly homogeneous classes usually are composed of students who carry different assumptions and who have varied cultural backgrounds and experiences. Have students practice analyzing arguments in class, and they'll probably encounter a broad range of knowledge, assumptions, and interpretations.

Stasis theory and the rhetorical appeals of ethos, pathos, and logos are powerful tools for understanding and creating arguments, but it may take students some time to sort them out. Students often rightly perceive the difficulty of separating the three appeals and treating them as distinct entities. In almost all rhetorical situations, the three appeals overlap significantly, so that, for example, an effective logical or emotional appeal builds a particular kind of ethos. They will also quickly realize that it can be difficult to find pure examples of the kinds of arguments that stasis theory introduces, but with work they should be able to see that many authors move through one or more stasis questions in making their arguments.

To help students understand stasis theory, you might consider walking through an imaginary crime in class. If someone goes missing, for example, there is a question of fact. Did something happen to this person? If a dead body is found, then investigators know that something happened and try to define the event: was it suicide, an accident, or a murder? If they can define the crime as murder, they might next evaluate it: was it murder in the first, second, or third degree? When they have evaluated the severity of the crime, the judicial system makes a proposal about what to do next: should the criminal be given a prison sentence of a limited number of years, life imprisonment, or the death penalty?

Not Just Words

Most students should be able to interpret a team shirt as an argument of loyalty or support, but it's worth asking them what the shirt says they support—is it an argument for a particular team, for the academic quality of the school, or even an argument against other particular schools (in the case of Arizona State, for example, the shirt might be an argument against the University of Arizona)? The pictured sweatshirt complicates things quickly. Not everyone who buys and wears this shirt will be associated with Arizona State, and the shirt's Victoria's Secret branding and the hearts around the Sun Devil suggest a sexually playful message. Most of all, think about this exercise as an opportunity to introduce students to the complexity of argument and help them see that contexts determine meaning.

Respond

1. Can an argument really be any text that expresses a point of view? What kinds of arguments—if any—might be made by the following items?
   - the embossed leather cover of a prayer book **[An expensive embossed leather cover might suggest that the text is held in high regard, arguing that the text deserves respect and attention.]**
   - a Boston Red Sox cap **[The cap can assert a fan's support for a baseball team and affirm a sense of identity with other fans, a city, even a region of the country. It could also be a taunt to fans of other teams, particularly the New York Yankees. It might also support the loyal tradition of Red Sox fans or celebrate their recent World Series wins.]**
   - a Livestrong bracelet **[The bracelet may argue that the wearer is committed to cancer-research charities or to fashionable trends.]**
   - the "explicit lyrics" label on a best-selling rock CD **[A label affixed to the CD might warn that the lyrics and themes in the album are unsuitable for children. Some people might avoid the CD for that reason, and others might select it because of the adult content.]**
   - the health warning on a package of cigarettes **[The warning describes potential consequences of smoking; some consumers might decide not to buy the cigarettes as a result, and some might feel guilty about their purchase. This warning might also serve as a good example of a strong argument that nonetheless frequently fails to persuade.]**
   - a belated birthday card **[Such a card, often humorous, is frequently a plea for forgiveness or understanding, arguing that the sender deserves credit for remembering the birthday at all.]**
   - the nutrition label on a can of soup **[The label offers facts about the product that readers may interpret as an argument for or against buying it. For example, the calories or fat or sodium totals might be higher or lower than those of competing products.]**

- the cover of a science fiction novel **[The cover usually depicts a futuristic scene. The argument might be "buy me and learn more."]**
- a colored ribbon pinned to a shirt lapel **[The ribbon may suggest that the wearer holds certain values about politics—or fashion.]**
- a Rolex watch **[The watch might imply that the owner is wealthy and tasteful enough to select a much-admired, highly refined product, or it might argue that the owner wants to display his or her wealth as a mark of personal distinction.]**

2. This exercise will get your students writing early and require them to think seriously about the differences between the goals of arguments and about their active participation in building arguments every day. You might remind them that arguments about sports or music or arguments in text messages or posts to Facebook walls count, too; that is, one of the goals of this exercise is to remind students that everything's an argument.
3. This exercise asks students to practice categorizing arguments and gets them to think critically about what contexts determine an argument's success. You might ask them to work in pairs and groups on this exercise so that they will be more alert to the idea that an argument's success can depend in large part on the audience.
4. What common experiences—if any—do the following objects, brand names, and symbols evoke and for what audiences in particular?
   - a USDA organic label **[associated with healthy, environmentally friendly, and perhaps fresher-tasting food; for health-conscious consumers]**
   - the Nike swoosh **[associated with athletes and athleticism, commercialization, coolness, foreign factories; probably for youths and young adults, in particular, but also for athletic older consumers]**
   - the golden arches **[associated with fast and relatively inexpensive food, convenience, efficiency, commercialism, American cultural imperialism, obesity; for children and families, perhaps travelers]**
   - the Sean John label as seen on its Web site **[associated with urban style and hip-hop culture; for young, fashion-conscious consumers, particularly African Americans]**

- a can of Coca-Cola **[associated with refreshment, relaxation, tradition, the necessity of caffeine, holidays, or U.S. power and cultural hegemony; for a worldwide audience]**
- Sleeping Beauty's castle on the Disney logo **[associated with childhood stories, wonder, magic, entertainment, Florida vacations, corporate power; for children and families, with an especially nostalgic appeal to adults]**
- Oprah Winfrey **[associated with sensitivity, self-empowerment, success, generosity, perhaps emotional manipulation; particularly successful with female audiences but with a broad American appeal]**
- the Vietnam Veterans Memorial **[associated with a divisive war, the honor accorded those killed in the war, and attempts to help heal the divisions created by the war; for those close to soldiers who died and for the country at large]**
- Ground Zero at the World Trade Center site **[associated with tragedy, loss, heroism, resilience; for those who lost a loved one on 9/11 and for the country at large]**
- a dollar bill **[associated with U.S. government, capitalism, enterprise, fiscal stability, aspiration, greed; for Americans but also some other nationalities, who may see the dollar as a threat from U.S. power or as a symbol of opportunity and success]**

5. Read the main editorial in three or four issues of your campus newspaper. Then choose the most interesting one, and consider how the editor creates credibility, or ethos, in the editorial. **[Answers will vary. If your school lacks a student paper, you might consider having students select editorials from a variety of publications, making sure that some students choose editorials from publications targeted toward young readers or another specialized audience. Students can then discuss how authors use different strategies for creating ethos. For example, an editorial writer in a music magazine directed toward young readers will employ ethos-building strategies significantly different from those an editorialist for the *Wall Street Journal* would use.]**
6. Take a look at the bumper sticker below, and then analyze it. What is its purpose? What kind of argument is it? Which of the stasis questions does it most appropriately respond to? What appeals

does it make to its readers, and how? **[This bumper sticker makes an appeal to values by asking us to think carefully about how we define patriotism and how the choice of what we drive has larger effects. Encourage your students to think about the ethos of a person who might put this bumper sticker on a car and the ways that images and words make its argument.]**

CHAPTER 2

Arguments Based on Emotion: Pathos

The "conceptual mess" of argument and persuasion that we discussed in Chapter 1 grows messier here: if argument is primarily a form of reasoned inquiry, what is the role of emotion in a responsible argument? Students will certainly struggle, as we all do, with distinguishing between appropriate and inappropriate emotion since that distinction is determined by the rhetorical situation, especially the audience. Determining appropriate and inappropriate emotion requires judgment, and agreement is never guaranteed.

Students may also struggle with distinguishing between reason and emotion. This chapter includes excerpts from emotionally grounded arguments that are effective *because* they exist on the shifting border between emotion and reason (think of how Georgina Kleege uses the fact of her blindness to make an emotional appeal) (p. 45). You can help your students see the relationships among reason, emotion, argument, and persuasion by drawing on the board a diagram that shows rational argument as a subset of persuasion. Invite your students to help you develop another diagram that shows *everything* as an argument.

Such a diagram leaves room for emotional appeals as a legitimate part of argument and inquiry, an idea that some students resist. Before you show the diagram, though, you might have your students develop their own diagrams to illustrate the relationships. Have the class critique those student diagrams as tests: where, for example, do the civil rights arguments of Martin Luther King Jr. fit in? (See pp. 179–80 for excerpts from his "I Have a Dream" speech.) How about Steve Jobs's appeals to a commencement audience? Under what conditions do these and other examples serve as legitimate argument?

Not Just Words

This image of the flag with corporate logos in place of the stars may strike many students as offensive, but they may not be able to articulate exactly why. First make sure that they can explain what argument the image is making. Many college students are not familiar with protests against corporate power, and the purpose of the image may confuse them.

If the students are bothered by this flag, press them to discuss what makes this image troubling for them: what values and emotions does this particular representation of the flag challenge? You can extend the consideration of this image by discussing whether appropriating an image like the flag is ever appropriate for protest or for support. How could they adapt the imagery of the flag to express their opinions about the United States?

Respond

1. To what specific emotions do the following slogans, sales pitches, and maxims appeal?
   - "Just do it." (ad for Nike) **[appeal to pleasure, boldness]**
   - "Think different." (ad for Apple computers) **[appeal to pride, creativity]**
   - "Reach out and touch someone." (ad for AT&T) **[appeal to love, joy, and pleasure]**
   - "Yes we can!" (2008 presidential campaign slogan for Barack Obama) **[appeal to hope, optimism, and community]**
   - "Country first." (2008 presidential campaign slogan for John McCain) **[appeal to patriotism and duty]**
   - "By any means necessary." (rallying cry from Malcolm X) **[appeal to fear or anxiety]**
   - "Have it your way." (slogan for Burger King) **[appeal to freedom, pleasure]**
   - "You can trust your car to the man who wears the star." (slogan for Texaco) **[appeal to anxiety, attachment, and security]**
   - "It's everywhere you want to be." (slogan for Visa) **[appeal to pleasure, anxiety, or security]**

- "Know what comes between me and my Calvins? Nothing!" (tag line for Calvin Klein jeans) **[appeal to pleasure]**
- "Don't mess with Texas!" (antilitter campaign slogan) **[appeal to fear and empathy]**

2. Most students can readily appreciate the connections between rhetoric and advertising, so asking them to determine how advertising employs rhetorical strategies can be an especially productive exercise. You might emphasize how different advertisers focus on different emotions. A magazine like *Spin*, aimed at a younger demographic than *Time*, is more likely to contain humorous advertisements. Ads in *Time* and *Newsweek* might appeal to the emotions that parents feel about their children since those magazines have an older audience.

3–4. These exercises ask students to think about arguments based on emotion in contexts that they might be more familiar with. For example, many students have probably noticed the difficulty of conveying tone and emotion in email and text messages, so they use emoticons and other signals (e.g., an abbreviation such as LOL) to signal emotional claims to their audiences. Humor in argument can make for good presentations and encourages students to think critically about texts that they encounter every day.

If you'd like to examine the use of emotional arguments over a longer period of time, you might ask students to do some research. Ask them to find texts of powerful speeches, such as Pericles's Funeral Oration, Martin Luther King Jr.'s "I Have a Dream," or Ronald Reagan's State of the Union addresses. Ask students to identify the emotional appeals *and* the logical appeals and to explain their combined effectiveness.

CHAPTER 3

Arguments Based on Character: Ethos

Aristotle says in the *Rhetoric* that the most important of the three proofs (logical, pathetic, ethical) is the argument based on character: if the audience does not trust the orator, all else is in vain. This chapter presents two primary difficulties for students. First, many students feel uncomfortable with the idea that ethos is context specific. They do not like the idea that good and honorable people can seek to change their self-presentation for different audiences without lying or misrepresenting themselves. Further, the idea that, say, Jessica Simpson has a more credible ethos than a senator or governor in the right context—for example, a cosmetics advertisement—bothers some students. Once they grasp the idea that context determines an argument's success, this idea that ethos can be elastic makes more sense.

The second and more important difficulty is that some first-year students find it a challenge to take on a voice they are not accustomed to and call it their own. Many students simply do not have the writing experience to believe that they have more than one voice or that they could develop a variety of voices for different rhetorical contexts.

Some students will want to argue that adopting different voices is a form of lying—by creating characters that do not exist or by taking on authority that is not theirs to claim.

Explain to students that the written voices they use in class, in emails to family members, and in job applications, for example, already differ, but that they are not necessarily false representations. Instead, each of these three kinds of writing attempts to create a character that foregrounds certain elements of students' interests and expertise and backgrounds others.

Not Just Words

For this exercise you might ask students to focus on the "Know Us" tab for Tata Motors, the "About Us" tab for the Global Compact, and the "About This Blog" section for Global Compact Critics. These areas of the Web sites give readers an indication of how these organizations mean to build and control their ethos. Students can then, in addition to evaluating the ethos of each site, analyze how well the Web sites meet the stated goals of each organization.

Once the students have created images for each of the organizations, push them to explain their choices carefully; presenting these images to others should help them understand that we don't all necessarily look for the same kinds of ethos in a car company—some may prefer environmental responsibility to performance, for example—or in a political organization.

Respond

1. Consider the ethos of each of the following public figures. Then describe one or two public arguments, campaigns, or products that might benefit from their endorsements as well as several that would not. **[Answers will vary; some suggestions are provided.]**
   - Oprah Winfrey—TV celebrity **[The popular host appeals especially to women, but her appeal is probably as broad as anyone's in America; her caring, generous, trustworthy demeanor means that she could sell almost anything and could have serious political influence as well.]**
   - Margaret Cho—comedian **[The outspoken comedian may offend many audiences, especially conservative audiences, with her politically charged humor. Her sympathy with gay, lesbian, bisexual, and transgender issues and her directness in talking about racial stereotypes and her own Asian American background have made her extremely popular in some minority communities.]**

- Kate Winslet—actress **[The popular actress could capitalize on her beauty and sell fashion and cosmetics to young women, but the wide acclaim she has received as a serious actress also suggests that she could be influential in promoting politics.]**
- Colin Powell—former chair of the Joint Chiefs of Staff and Secretary of State in the Bush administration **[The highly respected military and political leader has stature as a sober, mature, and experienced leader, which might lead to selling insurance or investments; he probably would not sell everyday consumer goods like laundry detergent; he might be very successful as a spokesperson for civic or educational initiatives.]**
- Sarah Palin—former Alaska governor and Republican vice-presidential candidate **[The charismatic politician has been wildly popular with conservative audiences but dismissed as a lightweight by many on the Left. She often mentions her role as a mother, and her experience as the mother of a child with Downs syndrome might make her a good spokesperson for issues concerning special-needs children.]**
- Dave Chappelle—humorist and columnist **[The edgy comedian includes plenty of pointed social and political satire in his show, as well as some drug humor; he probably should not sell serious products like life insurance but has enormous appeal to young audiences.]**
- Jeff Gordon—NASCAR champion **[The highly successful, photogenic NASCAR racer is controversial because he's a non-Southerner in a heavily Southern sport and because he looks less masculine than most NASCAR drivers; he could (and does) sell many products such as milk, Pepsi, and car-related products; he probably has little clout in political campaigns but might work as a spokesperson for worthy causes.]**
- Nancy Pelosi—speaker of the U.S. House of Representatives **[The first female speaker of the House seems to have become something of a polarizing figure; she has great appeal to liberal and progressive audiences but has become a target for conservatives. She would have great authority speaking on issues such as gender in politics,**

and many would respect her historical position as first female leader of the House.]

- Bill O'Reilly—TV news commentator **[The aggressive, opinionated talk-show host works for the Fox News Channel; he usually advocates conservative causes with appeals to a blue-collar background and populist ethos; he probably should not endorse luxury goods or products that might seem frivolous.]**
- Marge Simpson—sensible wife and mother on *The Simpsons* **[The generally responsible cartoon housewife occasionally goes off the deep end and often appears naïve; she could be an advocate for any number of mainstream products but is not likely to represent upscale or serious e.g., life insurance products.]**
- Jon Stewart—host of *The Daily Show* on Comedy Central **[Extremely popular with young, liberal, and progressive audiences, Stewart occupies an odd space—some audiences would take him seriously as a straightforward voice of reason while others would dismiss him as fundamentally unserious because he hosts a fake news show.]**

2–4. You might use these exercises to emphasize how different audiences and different contexts lead to different strategies for building credibility and enhancing ethos. Exercise 3 would be an especially good exercise for challenging students to think of situations where public figures they do not like could still be authoritative. Exercise 4 will push students to think creatively about how things that seem like flaws can actually be strengths. You can extend the exercises in this chapter by asking students to list the many voices they have and the situations in which they are appropriate. Ask students to find things they have written for different audiences, or assign them a topic and a set of audiences. For example, have them write three emails announcing that they've been dismissed from school. How is it different to write this news to one's parents, one's best friend, one's high school teachers,or one's siblings? (Note that this assignment asks most students to assume a voice they can't imagine actually needing to assume.) Once they've written their samples, ask the students to find and annotate the textual cues that demonstrate shifting rhetorical ethos.

CHAPTER 4

Arguments Based on Facts and Reason: Logos

Finally, the good stuff: evidence, facts, testimony, statistics—real numbers, real facts, and no more opinions and feelings. That's the attitude some first-year student writers will take. Students who feel lost without "solid facts" to support arguments will be happy to come to this chapter. But using evidence responsibly is complicated. Students will need to become comfortable critiquing facts as well as opinions, questioning surveys and statistical evidence, and uncovering assumptions that lie behind enthymemes. For example, you might introduce the factual claim that the Bayer company used to use in its aspirin advertising: "Nothing works better than Bayer." It's a fact: no aspirin works better than Bayer aspirin. But it's a fact that conceals the important point that other aspirins work equally well.

The concept of the arguable proposition might help students see that making a distinction between fact and opinion can sometimes be difficult. Certain propositions are not arguable: the square root of 81 is 9; Spain borders Portugal; Charles Dickens wrote in English. We do not argue about these claims because we accept them as commonplaces: they are, for most purposes, facts. But other facts are arguable: Christopher Columbus discovered America, William Shakespeare wrote all the plays attributed to him, clear-cutting in the rain forest has little environmental impact. At some point in the not-too-distant past, these last three facts were commonplaces, at least to certain audiences. But now they are arguable propositions: reasonable people could dispute the claims and offer other evidence in support of counterarguments.

Not Just Words

Students might have a hard time taking this poster seriously enough to see the possibility of logical arguments. Some possibilities for the argument that the poster is making include an attack on the corporate values that reduce motivation to snappy catchphrases, an attack on the idea that quality is a competition, or an attack on unreasonable or irrational goals.

It might be dangerous to direct students (or yourself) to the Web site that hosts the gallery of these posters because they're addictive and because a few aren't quite appropriate for class, but you might ask them to consider other posters in this series to see which parody offers the most logical caption. If there is time, you might also ask students to write their own captions for some of the images to see how well they can balance logical claims with humor.

Respond

1. Discuss whether the following statements are examples of hard evidence **[inartistic]** or rational appeals **[artistic]**. Not all cases are clear-cut.
   - The bigger they are, the harder they fall. **[artistic]**
   - Drunk drivers are involved in more than 50 percent of traffic deaths. **[inartistic; ask students to discuss how the word "involved" works in this claim.]**
   - DNA tests of skin found under the victim's fingernails suggest that the defendant was responsible for the assault. **[inartistic]**
   - Polls suggest that a large majority of Americans favor a constitutional amendment to ban same-sex marriage. **[inartistic]**
   - A psychologist testified that teenage violence could not be blamed on video games. **[inartistic]**
   - An apple a day keeps the doctor away. **[artistic]**
   - History proves that cutting tax rates increases government revenues because people work harder when they can keep more of what they earn. **[both]**
   - The only thing we have to fear is fear itself. **[artistic]**

- Air bags ought to be removed from vehicles because they can kill young children and small-framed adults. **[inartistic]**

2. Answers will vary, but most students will see that Rudner expects us to be familiar with Picasso's artistic style, especially his Cubist work, which broke figures apart into shapes. You might push them to treat this enthymeme like the canceled picnic example on p. 86 and ask them to come up with a list of the implied cultural information in this enthymeme (e.g., we expect cosmetic surgery to make us more attractive). The humor comes, at least in part, from the idea that the doctor's taste in art might represent his or her vision of human beings and/or the idea that a surgeon might take the same kind of artistic liberties that a painter would.

3–5. This chapter distinguishes between artistic and inartistic proofs: the first relies on authorial invention (enthymemes, syllogisms, analogies, and so on), and the second on specific pieces of evidence. Our experience has been that first-year writers are drawn to the inartistic appeals out of a belief that nothing convinces like hard evidence—the "facts" that seem inarguable. You will need to help your students see the effectiveness of artistic appeals, too. We offer several excerpts that you could use to explore artistic appeals, but a quick look at any newspaper op-ed page will reveal many more examples. As an introduction to Toulmin logic and as evidence for the idea that artistic appeals can be effective, have your students find the claims and reasons embedded in newspaper editorials. Student newspapers also offer, in our experience, examples of *ineffective* artistic appeals. First-year writers are usually able to explain what has gone wrong in an unpersuasive opinion piece, and you could profitably steer class discussion to the author's use of evidence.

CHAPTER 5

Rhetorical Analysis

This chapter puts together many principles from earlier chapters and asks students to use those principles as analytical tools. (The next few chapters emphasize how rhetoric can help them produce arguments.) The rhetorical concepts that the book has introduced help students to understand how and why people make the arguments that they do. First-year writers, who bring a range of experiences and abilities to the classroom, may know some of these concepts under different names. "Making a claim," for example, could be the equivalent of "writing a thesis." "Giving an argument shape" might be understood as "organizing." Students probably also can make sense of the differences between claims of emotion, character, and fact: they see such claims every day, and learning to think rhetorically can be understood as a way of organizing and commenting on ideas that they intuitively grasp. But once they can articulate these ideas, they can think, read, and write more consciously and critically.

Encourage your students to explore their familiarity with these concepts by asking them to name examples of each of the categories of argument. Popular advertisements are a good tool for showing students the power of carefully crafted appeals; students have sometimes studied advertisements in psychology classes, and they come to think of advertising as a series of tricks. But rhetorical analysis can help them see advertising—and therefore many other forms of discourse—as communication that they can understand. And what they can understand in others' arguments they can apply to their own.

Not Just Words

This exercise helps reveal how powerful a rhetorical analysis can be. Some students may feel energized by the idea that they can discover hidden agendas through the application of rhetorical concepts.

It's worth discussing the effectiveness of the claims made by zombietime.com and by the *San Francisco Chronicle*. Is Zombietime right that this picture reveals an "insidious" bias? And is the *Chronicle* really addressing the quality of its ethos, which is what Zombietime ultimately attacks? A careful discussion of the sample should help students make their own arguments about the images that they find.

Students are frequently adept at reading visual arguments, but they haven't had much practice paying attention to individual elements of argument inside those texts. Having students present their rhetorical analysis of the photo to the class will force them to articulate how they broke the text down into individual elements.

Respond

1. Describe a persuasive moment that you can recall from a speech, an article, an editorial, an advertisement, a video clip, or your personal experiences. Alternatively, research one of the following famous moments of persuasion, and describe the circumstances of the appeal—the historical situation, the issues at stake, the purpose of the argument, and the reasons it is memorable.
   - Abraham Lincoln's "Gettysburg Address" (1863) **[the turning point of the American Civil War, a reaffirmation of core Union values]**
   - Elizabeth Cady Stanton's draft of the "Declaration of Sentiments" for the Seneca Falls Convention (1848) **[a key statement of principles and arguments for women's rights]**
   - Franklin Roosevelt's first inaugural address (1933) **[an attempt by a new president to give Americans hope during the Great Depression]**
   - Winston Churchill's addresses to the British people during the early stages of World War II (1940) **[an attempt to rally a nation against a Nazi military onslaught threatening Britain]**

- Martin Luther King Jr.'s "Letter from Birmingham Jail" (1963) **[an attempt to remind white Christian leaders of the religious roots of the civil rights movement and to defend the principles of nonviolent civil disobedience]**
- Ronald Reagan's tribute to the *Challenger* astronauts (1986) **[a eulogy for the astronauts killed in the explosion of the space shuttle and an argument for continuing space exploration]**
- Toni Morrison's speech accepting the Nobel Prize (1993) **[an assertion of a feminist, African American presence in literature and theory]**
- Barack Obama's "A More Perfect Union" speech on race (2008) **[a response to the threat of scandal over his relationship with the controversial Rev. Jeremiah Wright and a call for Americans to recognize and reconcile racial divisions]**

2–4. These exercises ask a great deal of students and could easily serve as paper assignments. One of the most difficult aspects of a rhetorical analysis is that after students work hard to pull apart the different aspects of an argument, they're asked to put them all back together to make a judgment on the argument's overall effectiveness. Make sure that your students choose clearly argumentative texts to analyze. Though it's certainly possible to present an excellent rhetorical analysis of a news article, that may be a more challenging assignment than most first-year writing students should take on for their first rhetorical analysis. You might consider taking any one of these exercises and modeling the response for your class to help build their confidence before they begin their own rhetorical analyses.

CHAPTER 6

Academic Arguments

This chapter should help students sort out questions of goals, tone, format, and style that help them understand the expectations of college writing that they face in your class and, especially, in other classes that do not make their writing expectations quite as explicit.

Even though the standards for academic argument are high, students shouldn't be intimidated by the prospect of writing for academic audiences. It might be useful to remind students that they do not have to become the world's expert on a particular topic to display an appropriate and impressive level of expertise.

You might also stress with students that academic argument is not merely a set of tricks and steps like avoiding contractions and split infinitives—two grammatical points that students have often learned as hallmarks of formal writing—but instead a way of thinking seriously and responsibly about almost any topic. You may not need to spend a great deal of time on this chapter, but students will surely return to it again and again; they will probably find the criteria for academic argument listed on p. 139 and the model arguments particularly helpful in their own writing.

Not Just Words

You might expand this exercise into a requirement for one of the papers you assign. Have students include an image in the paper—be sure to remind them that a graph or a table is also a visual representation of information and that they don't have to limit themselves to a picture—and then have them attach a short appendix or addendum in which they explain how the image enhances their argument and why they chose that particular image. Encourage them to review Chapter 14 on visual arguments before they write their explanation.

Respond

1. **Answers will vary. You may need to help students locate appropriate academic arguments. If possible, consider devoting some class time to showing students how to access scholarly databases on a library Web site, or consider scheduling a workshop with a reference librarian if that option is available.**
2. Look closely at the following five passages, each of which is from an opening of a published work, and decide which ones provide examples of academic argument. How would you describe each one, and what are its key features? Which is the most formal and academic? Which is the least? How might you revise them to make them more—or less—academic?

   Judith Thurman establishes her authority by reviewing what is known about the topic of cave paintings but does not seek to create new knowledge about the topic. Thurman uses a clear and formal style and makes mostly logical appeals. Including more formal citations would make this argument more academic.

   Harry Crews is authoritative and uses a clear style, but he's writing about the topic of hitchhiking informally and not seeking to write about the topic in the way that, say, an academic sociologist might. To revise this into a more academic argument, a writer would more clearly identify what issues are at stake for a group of experts, seek out other sources besides personal experience, and opt for a more formal tone.

   Elizabeth Derse's study of nitrogen sources is the most academic of the five passages, meeting all the criteria for academic argument listed on p. 139. To revise the text into a less academic argument, a writer might offer a narrative that details personal experiences exploring and researching coral reefs, eliminate academic sources and citations, and perhaps use more emotional appeals about the importance of coral reefs and the dangers of degradation.

   Kay S. Hymowitz's editorial is probably the least academic of the group (some might say that Crews is the least academic). Her argument relies heavily on emotional appeals based on personal preference, employs an informal tone, and does not focus on an issue as it would interest ac-

ademic peers. To revise this argument into a more academic piece, a writer might shift the emphasis to a concern such as young women, body image, and self-display; focus on incorporating more logical appeals; and opt for a more formal tone.

Dagoberto Gilb's argument is relatively informal, does not seek to deal evenhandedly with an opposing point of view, and relies heavily on emotional appeals. To revise this into a more academic argument, a writer might review what is known about the topic in a less partisan way, include more logical appeals based on research, and establish a more authoritative ethos.

3. Read the following paragraphs, and then list changes the writer might make to convert them into an academic argument.

   The writer might approach this topic from a more academic point of view by reviewing academic opinions about cultural uniformity (rather than remarks from interviews and nonacademic writings), employing a more formal style (for example, omitting the joke about hell at the end of the second paragraph), providing evidence of more rigorous research about the presence of chain stores, and/or including citations of sources used to build the argument.

4–5. **Answers will vary.**

CHAPTER 7

Structuring Arguments

We all need help structuring arguments, so be ready to spend some time on this chapter. Even many of the strongest first-year writers have only one model, the five-paragraph essay, for organizing their writing. Too often, that model is overly rigid for them; they focus on counting paragraphs rather than using the format as a way of shaping an argument. The classical oration will not be a big leap for those who know the five-paragraph model, and it might help some students realize that the important concept for organizing their essays is working through the logic of the claim, not just filling in the required number of sentences and paragraphs.

Rogerian argument and Toulmin logic will likely prove more difficult for students to master. With Rogerian rhetoric, the key idea will be the importance of taking opposing positions seriously and treating them fairly. For many students, political argument, particularly the zero-sum arguments of political elections, provides the primary model for thinking about argument and persuasion. But in academic argument, which is the writing that most students will be doing in the next few years, the goal of an argument might be better understood as entering a conversation and modifying or refining other positions, not defeating the competition and winning an argument.

Toulmin logic can seem complicated at first—so many concepts, so many terms. But for reasons that we explain in the chapter, Toulmin logic can also be powerful as an analytic and productive tool. Our experience has been that when first-year students commit themselves to understanding and using the Toulmin framework, their writing improves noticeably. Students begin to make arguments that use evidence effectively, and they write papers that show greater sensitivity to audience. The system holds students accountable for every part of their argument, while forcing them to question the foundations and assumptions underlying their claims.

But like any complicated system, Toulmin logic takes time to learn. Do not expect your students to become comfortable with the concepts immediately. Instead, plan to introduce and review the various elements of Toulmin argument over a period of weeks. Take your time leading students through the idea of claims and reasons. These two key elements might take a week to explain completely, especially if you use real-world examples in which claims and reasons are not made explicit. (Letters to the editor of any newspaper will illustrate the problems of making clear claims supported by coherent reasons. Some letters will serve as examples of good, clear writing; others will make great counterexamples.)

Students usually struggle with the idea that there are two kinds of evidence—in support of reasons and of warrants—and that an argument might be exemplary in its use of one while completely ignoring the other. The Toulmin system gives you a way of explaining to your students exactly what the evidentiary problems are in their arguments. You can praise a student's use of statistical evidence in support of the reasons, for instance, while asking him or her to provide more evidence in support of the warrant. Our experience has been that when students come to understand the distinction between these two forms of evidence, they also learn to create more effective enthymemes: students can work backward from evidence to claims.

Not Just Words

Because these Web sites update frequently, we can't predict how Rogerian the arguments will be when you and your students encounter them. As this book goes to press, Al Gore's "We" site seems to employ more language that focuses on mutual understanding and cooperation, but you might point out to students that the language of cooperation tends to come up more frequently in the party that holds political power; those in power can afford to be more magnanimous and talk about the importance of cooperation.

You might expand this exercise to discuss the strengths and limitations of Rogerian argument. Almost every politician claims to believe in compromise and cooperation, but do students believe that it would truly benefit us if Rogerian rhetoric were the model for our political discourse? Do the students find it personally appealing? Do they trust politicians who employ it? An interesting exercise might be to perform an analysis of the Declaration of Independence—where do we see Jefferson employing Rogerian strategies? Where do we see him abandoning them? How does his particular mix of argumentative strategies work?

Respond

1. Answers will vary. You might use this exercise to reinforce the idea of the importance of argument structure. For example, if a student chooses a controversial issue such as abortion, Rogerian argument would probably not be a good choice for an audience of true believers on either side of the issue.
2. Following is a claim with five possible supporting reasons. State the warrant that would support each of the arguments in brief. Which of the warrants would need to be defended? Which one would a college audience likely accept without significant backing? **[Answers will vary; some suggested warrants are offered.]**

   We should amend the Constitution to abolish the Electoral College

   - because a true democracy is based on the popular vote, not the votes of the usually unknown electors. **[True democracy should be our goal; true democracy does not rely on representatives to do the people's voting.]**
   - because under the Electoral College system the votes of people who have minority opinions in some states end up not counting. **[Minority opinions should count in every state; all votes should count equally.]**
   - because then Al Gore would have won the 2000 election. **[Al Gore would have been a better president than George W. Bush; Al Gore should have won the 2000 election.]**
   - because the Electoral College is an outdated relic of an age when the political leaders didn't trust the people. **[Outdated institutions need to be changed; political leaders should trust the people who vote.]**
   - because the Electoral College skews power toward small and midsize states for no good reason. **[The Electoral College**

disrupts the natural balance of power; there must be a good reason if power is going to be skewed toward small and midsize states.]

3–5. You can help students learn Toulmin logic by taking every opportunity to use the terminology in class. The more students hear the words, the more comfortable they will be using them themselves. (We have gone so far sometimes as to state *everything* in class as claim, reasons, and warrant: "Claim: Rob, you should help me arrange the desks in a circle. Reason: Because I want everyone to see each other in the discussion. Warrant: Seeing other students in a discussion is good. Warrant: If I want a student to do something in class, the student should do it." Or if a student says she is hungry, we restate it: "Claim: I am hungry. Reason: Because I have not eaten since last night.") Some students might complain about the complicated system. Help these students make their complaints using Toulmin logic: "Claim: I do not like learning Toulmin logic. Reason: Toulmin is too complicated." You can examine these claims, explore the reasons and warrants, and show your students why Toulmin will help them. In short, use the system to show how powerful it can be.

A final note: students work hard in other classes to learn complicated systems. Every academic field has terminology and a taxonomy that take time to learn. You should make no apologies for teaching difficult material. Toulmin is hard to learn, but the effort is repaid many times over. (Enthymeme: If students work hard to learn in any other classes, then they can expect to work hard to learn in a writing class, too.)

CHAPTER 8

Arguments of Fact

This is the first chapter that deals explicitly with the stases that were introduced in Chapter 1. The first stasis question in the ancients' tradition was of fact: did something happen? Before an argument can progress to the next stage, everyone must agree that something did happen. Consider a missing person case. If no one knows where the person is and no body can be found, then authorities cannot arrest and try someone for murder, decide that an accident occurred, or rule the death a suicide. First, there must be agreement that something happened; only after the parties have agreed that *something* has happened can they determine which term or definition best applies. An argument of fact is the basis of further claims.

Your students may find arguments of fact to be especially interesting because they have long understood facts to be immutable. Problems arise, however, when they begin to consider what kinds of facts can be reasonably argued and which cannot be reasonably argued. There's no easy answer to this question. For instance, consider the statement that there has only been one Roman Catholic president of the first forty-four; such a claim hardly seems arguable. A quick look in any encyclopedia would confirm this fact. But what if a historian found evidence that an earlier president was a Roman Catholic who had suppressed his religious affiliation because he feared the anti-Catholic prejudice that was common in the late nineteenth century? In that case, even this seemingly straightforward, easily verified claim becomes arguable. A good argument with good evidence can make new facts.

This example, which falls far afield from the work that students will produce in their classes, nonetheless might help them understand that facts can be arguable. They may, however, find it difficult to come up with topics of their own that are manageable in the papers they'll be writing for class. Research will play a crucial role in developing good factual arguments, and the brainstorming exercises included below should help them sort out which arguments would be particularly viable for a paper.

Not Just Words

The visual presentation of information in graphs and charts asks students to read in a different way. To extend this exercise, you might ask students to find examples of arguments made visually that mislead the viewer. You might also spend some time looking at the different graphs that appear in *USA Today.* You might then have the students compare those graphs to the mock graphics that the satirical newspaper the *Onion* (www.theonion.com) includes on its front page.

Respond

1. For each topic in the following list, decide whether the claim is worth arguing to a college audience, and explain why or why not: **[Answers will vary; some suggestions are provided.]**
   - Hurricanes are increasing in number and ferocity. **[Worth arguing; how far back does reliable data reach? How well could we measure hurricane strength before the Saffir-Simpson scale was created? How do we compare hurricanes that are now hitting populated coastal areas to those that hit coastal areas with few residents?]**
   - Many people die annually of cancer. **[Not worth arguing; the claim can be easily supported by one or two numbers.]**
   - Fewer people would die of heart disease each year if more of them paid attention to their diets. **[Probably worth arguing; though diet has long been considered a risk factor for heart disease, there might be contrary evidence.]**
   - Japan might have come to terms more readily in 1945 if the Allies hadn't demanded unconditional surrender. **[worth arguing]**
   - Boys would do better in school if there were more men teaching in elementary and secondary classrooms. **[worth arguing]**

- The economic recession will lead drivers to give up their gas-guzzling SUVs for more energy-efficient vehicles. **[worth arguing]**
- There aren't enough high-paying jobs for college graduates these days. **[Worth arguing; what constitutes enough? What do we consider high pay?]**
- Hydrogen may never be a viable alternative to fossil fuels because it takes too much energy to change hydrogen into a useable form. **[Worth arguing; how much energy is too much? What if we run out of fossil fuels or if obtaining them becomes too costly?]**
- Its opponents have grossly exaggerated the effects of the USA Patriot Act on free expression. **[worth arguing]**

2–4. These exercises would be especially useful for helping students brainstorm paper topics of their own. First-year writing students often find that it's difficult to come up with reasonable factual claims for short papers. You might use exercise 2 as group work in class. Immediate peer review of topic ideas will help some students see how reasonable their claims might be as well as how much work individual claims might require. Exercise 3 gives students a number of examples of factual arguments to look at as models. You might also direct them to www.snopes.com, a site that examines urban legends, for enjoyable examples of factual arguments.

CHAPTER 9

Arguments of Definition

A traditional legal example of stasis theory's practical application concerns a missing urn. This example works well in the classroom as an introduction to arguments of definition: an urn is discovered to be missing from a house and is found in the house of another person. At the level of fact, there is agreement: the defendant has the urn that belongs to the plaintiff. But there is considerable disagreement about definition: the plaintiff argues that the urn was stolen, whereas the defendant argues that it was merely *borrowed*. The case can go no further until the parties settle the question of definition. Only after the parties have defined "theft" and "borrowing" and only after they have determined which term best applies can the case move forward.

Toulmin logic will help you explain the contested, rhetorical nature of definitional claims. Because definitional criteria are warrants, they must be chosen with the audience in mind (if the audience members do not accept the criteria you choose, they will not accept any other part of the argument). You could return to the urn example to demonstrate the need for *shared* definitions of theft or borrowing. If, for example, you were to argue that borrowing without explicit permission constitutes theft, you would need to provide evidence for that criterion; your evidence must be tailored to a particular audience. Not everyone would accept that criterion: what about close friends who share their possessions without needing permission each time they borrow something?

Some students who struggle will be able to place an object within a given class (a fiddle is certainly a violin; prostitution is an exploitative business; paid workers are not volunteers) but will balk at the need to explore or defend definitional criteria. Turn to Toulmin to show that they might have evidence in support of their reasons but not in support of the warrants—the definitional criteria themselves.

Not Just Words

These images may not be straightforward for some students, but the conflicting definitions that your students pull out could lead to excellent class discussions. You might extend the exercise by asking students to bring or create images that illustrate their preferred definitions of patriotism. The adaptation of the Uncle Sam recruiting poster might be an especially interesting image to ask your students to work with. How might they appropriate this image to put forward their own definition of patriotism? You can have them describe how they might put together a poster of their own, but many of your students can manipulate images to create their own poster, so you might consider asking them to bring those images into class or to post them on the Web.

Respond

1. Briefly discuss the criteria that you might use to define the italicized terms in the following controversial claims of definition. Compare your definitions of the terms with those of your classmates. **[Answers will vary; some possibilities are offered.]**
   - Graphic novels are *serious literature.* **[must offer some psychological depth and some meaning beyond the surface; must be of high enough quality to be read for decades or centuries; must offer some kind of commentary on the human condition]**
   - Burning a nation's flag is a *hate crime.* **[must be a crime or prosecutable act; must be aimed at a specific group; must be intended to hurt, demean, or disparage]**
   - Conor Oberst defines *emo.* **[must include deeply personal lyrics; must explore a sense of poetic desperation in music; must take part in the larger world of emo fashion and trends in addition to creating or listening to the music]**
   - Matt Drudge and Arianna Huffington are *legitimate journalists.* **[must earn a living by reporting the news; must be**

trained in journalism either by schooling or through practical experience; must report the news ethically and responsibly]

- College sports programs have become *big businesses.* **[must generate considerable income; must be enterprises that aim at constant growth; must be regional or national in scope; must make decisions to ensure their own success or profit]**
- Plagiarism can be an act of civil *disobedience.* **[must be a conscious act of lawbreaking; must be an act intended to question the legitimacy of the law being broken; must be a violation with legal consequences; must be an act for which the perpetrator is willing to accept the consequences]**
- Satanism is a *religion* properly protected by the First Amendment. **[must be a set of beliefs about the ultimate meaning or focus of life; must have beliefs that are shared by a group; must have beliefs that have a bearing on the conduct of one's life]**
- Campaign contributions are acts of *free speech* that should not be regulated. **[must be an expression of an idea through language, written or oral; must be an expression of a political character or with a political interest; must be noncommercial and nonthreatening]**
- The District of Columbia should not have all the privileges of an American *state.* **[must be a discrete territory in a relationship with the United States of America; must be a territory of reasonable size; must be a unit with economic and social diversity; must have historical significance as a territory]**
- Gay and lesbian couples should have the legal privileges of *marriage.* **[must be an enduring bond between adults; must be a bond established to sustain family life; must be a sacramental bond; must be a sexual union]**

2–3. These exercises offer suggestions for helping students think of their own definitional claims by extending examples in the text. Another good exercise is for students to come up with far-fetched definitional claims: Oprah Winfrey is a cult leader; Disney is a virus; Tom Cruise is an alien. We've seen students write engaging, thoughtful arguments on these seemingly bizarre topics. Students often gravitate to topics such as capital punishment or abortion when writing definition arguments; however, when they approach the assignment more creatively, they seem to structure their arguments more effectively and develop their criteria in unexpected but reasonable ways. (An alien doesn't have to come from outer space, for example; maybe the world of celebrity that Tom Cruise inhabits is so different from ours that it may as well be an alien world.) When students write about the more creative claims and experiment with offbeat arguments, they have a greater opportunity to say something fresh.

CHAPTER 10

Evaluations

In the notes for Chapter 9, we explained the classic illustration of the missing urn: the urn belonging to one person is found in the home of another. The parties disagree about the nature of the incident. One says the urn was stolen, and the other says it was merely borrowed. The matter is stuck at the level of definition, but let's imagine that the court decides the urn was stolen. The defendant might argue that he stole the urn for a good reason: the urn contained water that he needed for his ill child. The defendant now makes an argument of evaluation: the act of theft was, he claims, praiseworthy.

You can use the story of the urn to show your students how arguments of evaluation grow out of arguments of definition. The transition from definition to evaluation can be tricky, however; as you're writing, it's not always clear when you're defining and when you're evaluating. (For example, if you define someone as a hero, isn't that also an evaluation?) Nevertheless, most students will benefit from thinking of the two as separate, at least in the abstract.

Many students will need help choosing the level of evaluative abstraction for their arguments. It's one thing to argue that *Raiders of the Lost Ark* is great art; it's something else to argue that it's a good Harrison Ford blockbuster. The best argument probably lies between those extremes, and most students will need help crafting a strong, arguable thesis. Some students will be content to argue that something is good or bad; push them to complicate their ideas so that they write more interesting arguments.

As with arguments of definition, evaluative arguments challenge students to defend their criteria. Toulmin logic will show that criteria are warrants and must be developed with audience in mind. If the audience does not accept the criteria, the evaluative judgment will not be accepted either. Peer review or other forms of draft response will provide students with an audience of thoughtful readers who might challenge writers' criteria.

Not Just Words

The power of a chart like this can perhaps best be understood in the way you might understand a Piet Mondrian painting: if you rearrange the given presentation, you change everything. Ask students how they might rearrange this chart. What information could they highlight or suppress? How might a supporter of the American effort in Iraq present the same information? You might ask students to research how political campaigns use charts and graphs to present information. How do they design visual information to make their arguments?

Respond

1. Choose one item from the following list that you understand well enough to evaluate. Develop several criteria of evaluation that you could defend to distinguish excellence from mediocrity in the area. Then choose an item that you don't know much about and explain the research you might do to discover reasonable criteria of evaluation for it. **[Answers will vary considerably. You might use this exercise as an in-class activity, having students work in groups according to which topics they know best. Many students will be surprised by how many criteria the group can come up with and how challenging it can be to establish criteria that many people can accept.]**
   - fashion designers
   - Navajo rugs
   - musicals
   - spoken word poetry
   - UN secretaries-general
   - NFL quarterbacks
   - social networking sites
   - TV journalists
   - video games
   - organic vegetables
   - animated films
   - universal health care plans

2–5. Exercises 2 through 5 highlight the importance of developing evaluative criteria, which in our experience has been the step that most frustrates students. Because students generally feel comfortable with evaluative arguments in some form (such as for movies and sports), they can usually generate topics and claims with ease. They tend to have more difficulty tailoring criteria to specific audiences. With supplementary exercises, therefore, we recommend that you focus on helping them think about the warrants for particular claims, a skill that they can then transfer to their papers.

CHAPTER 11

Causal Arguments

Causal arguments can be extremely challenging for students; the logic of causality is complex, the evidence is often shaky, and the results can be uncertain. In some versions of the stases, causal arguments came before arguments of evaluation; in others, they came after. Show your class (by using the examples from this book or from elsewhere) that regardless of their place in the order of the stases, causal arguments build on and set up other arguments. Like definitions and evaluations, they rarely appear in pure form, though we provide some examples of such pure causal arguments in the text. The situations that open the chapter suggest such ideal causal arguments, though they also rely on definitional issues.

We have found that students typically try to tackle causal arguments that reach too far for a regular class paper; it's too much to explain the effects of the French Revolution in four pages. Remember, too, that because the logic of causal arguments can be complex, students will likely benefit from extra time and help as they make causal claims. For useful models, you might turn to sports writing. Students can easily see how reasonable, informed observers can differ on why a team or an individual won or lost a competition.

Not Just Words

This exercise of picking out causal arguments will remind students that causal arguments are complex and must take into account a number of considerations. This exercise should also remind students how intertwined the stases are: a causal argument about the use of DDT will be tightly joined to an evaluation argument about whether the insecticide's use is a good idea. And, of course, these causal arguments strongly imply a proposal argument as well.

Respond

1. The causes of some of the following events and phenomena are quite well known and frequently discussed. But do you understand them well enough to spell out the causes to someone else? Working in a group, see how well (and in how much detail) you can explain each of the following events or phenomena. Which explanations are relatively clear, and which seem more open to debate?
   - earthquakes **[clear]**
   - the Burning Man festival **[open to debate]**
   - the collapse of communism in Eastern Europe in 1989 **[open to debate]**
   - arroyos **[clear]**
   - the AIDS pandemic in Africa **[open to debate]**
   - the popularity of the *Batman* films **[open to debate]**
   - the swelling caused by a bee sting **[clear]**
   - the mortgage crisis of 2008 and 2009 **[open to debate]**
   - the rise in cases of autism **[open to debate]**
   - the destruction of the space shuttle *Columbia* **[open to debate]**

2–4. Exercises 2 and 3 would work well as large-group activities. For exercise 2, go around the class several times to see how far afield from the initial cause you can go. Alternatively, go around the class only once for each cause, but choose several initial causes to take to extremes. Exercise 4, which offers students practice at differentiating between types of causes, would also make a good in-class exercise, though you might have students work individually or in pairs and then compare causal arguments.

CHAPTER 12

Proposals

This chapter provides students with the opportunity to put all their previous work in the service of a complex argument. Proposal arguments have been popular in our classes because most students see them as the culmination of the semester's effort: once students have learned to analyze and produce arguments of definition, evaluation, and causation, proposal arguments make more sense. You can ask students to define terms carefully, to explain their evaluative criteria, or to explore the causal connections more thoroughly. This is a fun unit to teach because students put their rhetorical training to use and use language to change the world. If you review the stases before you teach the proposal argument, students will understand that the proposal does not exist in a vacuum but instead builds on what's come before.

Students often enjoy writing about practical problems on campus or in the community. Policy issues can make good papers, too, though you'll want to be careful that students don't tackle too much: sometimes they try to resolve world hunger in five pages. If your students write policy proposals, be sure to teach them the dangers of biting off more than they can chew.

We have asked students in our classes to do extensive audience analysis as part of the writing process. The chapter's guide to writing proposal arguments gives students some ideas about audience analysis, but you can go beyond what we provide. In the early stages of the writing process, ask students to write about their audience and consider the approaches that will be most rhetorically effective. Remind your students that if a proposal is to be accepted, it needs to be finely tuned to the demands of its audience. Toulmin logic could help some students understand their audience by drawing attention to warrants.

Not Just Words

No other student-written argument seems to lend itself to a variety of student presentations as well as the proposal argument. This exercise asks students to think particularly about a local audience, perhaps their school or home community. Such a focus allows students to identify their audience's interests more specifically, which usually leads to much better arguments. Many of your students are likely to have highly developed technical skills, so you might consider requiring them to create Web sites for their proposal arguments. But you might also ask them to think about what kinds of proposal arguments might benefit from simpler, less technical presentations.

Respond

1. The most important aspect of this exercise lies in pushing students to move beyond relatively simple solutions. For instance, some students might suggest "more education about the dangers of obesity" as a way of addressing the increasing rate of obesity in the United States. We have no objections to more education, but encourage your students to make more specific proposals. "More education" and "better funding" are relatively common proposal arguments that need to be explained fully and thoughtfully to be persuasive.

2–3. The exercises focus on two key issues for proposal arguments: developing claims that represent responses to real problems and tailoring proposals to a specific audience. Extend the exercises by asking students to examine a variety of proposals—from editorials in the student newspaper to large-scale governmental policy proposals—in terms of those same issues. How have the writers of policy proposals identified a real problem that's worth solving? How have editorial writers targeted their audience in their proposals? Also, consider asking students to identify the proposals that might be hidden within other forms of argument: is the writer making a proposal without seeming to?

CHAPTER 13

Style in Arguments

Figurative language is so prevalent—we argue in the chapter that it is "indispensable to language use"—that students will be able to find and analyze examples of figures from almost any source. One of our students once wrote a paper about figurative language in country music; she had a hard time finding lyrics that *weren't* highly figurative, and she argued that country music wouldn't be country music without figures.

This chapter might best be approached as part of another unit so you can show the relationship between figures and definition, for example. Metaphor is a definitional argument, after all. By combining this chapter with others, you can illustrate the ways figures argue and are not merely dressing on top of already established arguments. You can also push students to think carefully about what tropes they can include in their own arguments. Too often, students do not think much about their style, in part because they don't have the means to understand how to write stylishly. Use this chapter to help them become more conscious about *how* they write.

Challenge your students to find figures or tropes that we have not listed in this chapter. They could do research into the ancient rhetorical terms, or they could develop their own. Give students a piece of writing that is rich with figurative language and ask them to identify each of the figures. Are there any sentences that seem to contain no schemes or tropes? Could it be that these sentences are figurative in ways students don't expect or recognize? Remind them that figures represent changes in the ordinary syntax or signification; how might these remaining sentences be read as different from the ordinary?

Not Just Words

We won't presume to predict just what the style of these pants indicates; you'll probably have a number of students who can articulate that far better than we could. Students who are alert to nuances of details in clothing can help the rest of the class understand the importance of details and presentation in writing.

A student who understands that we dress for a variety of reasons—not just to cover ourselves and not just for comfort—might be a little closer to understanding that we don't just always "say what we mean." The best arguments, like the best dressers, pay attention to style, which is more than just ornamentation, as this chapter explains. Style, in writing or in clothing, helps create meaning.

Respond

1, 2, 4, 5. These exercises ask students to become more conscious of style both as readers and as writers. These types of productive exercises are thousands of years old; students have been writing with schemes and tropes since at least the fifth century B.C. These kinds of exercises have persisted because they succeed—by helping students to recognize figurative language in others' sentences and to identify and use schemes and tropes more naturally in their own everyday writing.

3. In the following advertising slogans, identify the types of figurative language used—metaphor, simile, analogy, hyperbole, understatement, rhetorical question, antonomasia, irony, parallelism, antithesis, inverted word order, anaphora, or reversed structure.
   - "Good to the last drop." (Maxwell House Coffee) **[hyperbole]**
   - "It's the real thing." (Coca-Cola) **[antonomasia, understatement]**
   - "Melts in your mouth, not in your hands." (M&M's) **[parallelism]**
   - "Be all that you can be." (U.S. Army) **[reversed structure]**

- "Breakfast of champions." (Wheaties) **[hyperbole, antonomasia]**
- "Double your pleasure; double your fun." (Doublemint gum) **[parallelism]**
- "Got Milk?" (America's Milk Processors) **[rhetorical question]**
- "Let your fingers do the walking." (the Yellow Pages) **[metaphor]**
- "Think small." (Volkswagen) **[understatement]**
- "Like a Rock." (Chevy trucks) **[simile]**
- "Real bonding, real popcorn, real butter, real good times." (Pop-Secret Popcorn) **[anaphora]**

CHAPTER 14

Visual Arguments

As we suggested in earlier notes, most students are familiar with some techniques of visual argument even if they are not able to analyze those techniques critically. Images occupy such a large part of students' daily lives—in advertisements, on television, even in textbooks—that they are almost bombarded by visual arguments. But your students may need a framework for understanding such arguments so that they can review them critically in what they read and use them honestly in what they write.

This chapter offers that framework and takes a highly rhetorical approach to visual arguments. That is, the chapter does more than make recommendations about choosing fonts or effectively positioning items on a page (though it includes such advice as well); it also asks students to ponder the rhetorical impact of visual texts and images on readers.

The final sections of the chapter offer advice on reading and writing visual texts, as well as focus on rhetorical concepts. For instance, the elements of successful visual presentations are arranged according to the three appeals discussed earlier in the book so that writers are asked to consider visual arguments based on ethos, pathos, and logos. You might ask students to offer more examples of how these appeals translate when operating in highly visual texts such as advertisements or magazine covers. Indeed, magazine advertising is a rich source of visual arguments because almost all ads make the same claim: the reader should buy our product.

Once your class is comfortable analyzing advertisements, you could move on to other visual arguments, such as textbook illustrations, statistical charts and graphs, product logos, and photojournalism—all of which are visually represented in this chapter.

Not Just Words

This exercise presents images that many students will find familiar, but they might never have thought about stamps as a kind of argument before. The discussion of these stamps should be a productive classroom exercise. If you would like to extend the exercise, you might have students consider other stamps that are available at www.usps.com (especially the year's commemorative stamps), or you might have them look at stamps from other decades, easily found online. How do arguments about America change from decade to decade? Or have them look at international stamps: how do the arguments made by stamps in other countries differ from those of American stamps?

Respond

1–4. These exercises encourage students to write about visual images, a challenging task. Help your students develop a rich vocabulary of visual arguments by pointing them to the questions in the chapter under the heading "Analyzing Visual Elements of Arguments" (pp. 446–51) and by doing several sample analyses in class. Once students are comfortable thinking critically about images in class, they will be more able to go off on their own to do critical analyses. You could also bring to class examples of good writing about images: short pieces of art criticism, incisive movie reviews, columns by popular cultural critics, and so forth.

CHAPTER 15

Presenting Arguments

This chapter asks students to think about rhetoric as a set of tools that can help us shape our arguments in any number of different media. Help your students understand that audience awareness, style, and appeals to ethos, pathos, and logos are important means of persuasion in any argument.

Web sites present rich opportunities for rhetorical analysis: they usually contain textual and visual arguments; their organization can differ radically from print texts; and they face a potentially worldwide audience. But when students make their own arguments in electronic environments, the tools of rhetoric will guide their decisions.

This chapter also offers a rhetorical approach to spoken arguments. Writing courses are increasingly being called on to address speaking abilities, and persuasive, skillful oral presentation needs to be learned and practiced as surely as written presentation does. Even when you're not working on oral presentations, you might ask students to read aloud some of their work or sample arguments from other sources. Ask students to read carefully, perhaps even somewhat dramatically. They'll learn a great deal about how style helps create an argument, and you'll benefit from learning more about how they hear language.

Not Just Words

You might give students the option or even the requirement that they present one of their arguments for your class in a format other than a traditional essay. In particular, proposal arguments, which often come last in a writing class, lend themselves to a wide variety of formats. Asking students to consider alternative means of presentation almost always forces them to think more fully about the audience to whom they might address their arguments, a step that often results in higher-quality work.

Respond

1–4. For exercise 1, make sure that students take no more than four paragraphs of a written essay to work with. You might suggest that they enlarge the type and increase the line spacing when they rewrite the text for oral argument. These changes will allow the student to highlight certain words and insert reminders to pause or slow down, ask for questions, or offer extratextual comments. Exercises 2, 3, and 4 ask students to examine other arguments and figure out what makes them successful or unsuccessful. Have students bring their notes on these other arguments to class and work in small groups to discover what similarities or differences in strategies they identified. Were the strategies and their successes determined by audience, personal preference, or something else?

CHAPTER 16

What Counts as Evidence

This can be a fun chapter for first-year writers, who, in our experience, believe that "real" evidence is always statistical or quantitative. When you show your students that they have a wide range of sources and forms available to them, their arguments will probably improve. As with some of the other chapters in Part 4, this chapter might be best taught in conjunction with a larger unit: combine a discussion of evidence with an assignment to write an evaluative argument, for instance.

Once you explain to your class that evidence can take many forms, you can move on to a discussion of the inventional role evidence can take: finding one piece of evidence can lead students not just to other pieces of evidence but also to new ways of making their arguments. Searching for evidence in libraries, interviews, or observations is not simply a one-way activity that goes from one source to the next. Instead, it can help students understand what claims they want to make, how they can approach the argument, and how they should tailor their arguments to an audience.

First-year writers have often not yet chosen a major, but they might have some interest in a particular field or discipline. You could ask your students to interview faculty in their chosen field to find out what counts as evidence in that discipline. Students could then present their findings to the class. This is a two-part lesson: students have to *find* evidence *about* evidence.

Not Just Words

This exercise argues for the power of visual images by having students discuss what would be lost if we had only verbal descriptions of what the children drew. But it's also likely to challenge our understanding of what constitutes authoritative evidence. How often do we look to something like children's artwork as evidence for political crimes? In what circumstances do we trust children more than, say, official reports? What are the costs or dangers of relying on children's reports of their experiences? You might also ask students to think creatively about what kinds of evidence they could use in their own projects, especially proposal arguments, which are often about local and community issues.

Respond

1–3. These exercises focus on the inventional role of evidence gathering, not just the technical questions of how to find evidence. It's important to discuss the limits of certain forms of evidence, as well as their strengths. Exercise 3, in which students observe another class, gives you an opportunity to talk about the limits of observations and field notes. You could develop other limit-setting exercises for other forms of evidence.

If you'd like to teach your students research techniques, you might think of scheduling a day in the library to walk around the reference areas and experiment with the catalog. Ask the librarians if they offer a guided tour or tutorial for students. Technical research skills are valuable, and first-year students rarely learn them except in their writing classes.

CHAPTER 17

Fallacies of Argument

Our experience has been that first-year writers can really do well in a unit on fallacies. They enjoy finding the fallacies in newspaper editorials, Web pages, and even their own papers (it's a little embarrassing to have fallacious reasoning pointed out, but students usually appreciate the help). And searching for fallacies can be like a treasure hunt: you know you're going to find something somewhere, but you don't know what or where.

The fallacies we've listed here constitute only a few of the many that logicians and rhetoricians have identified through the years. You could ask your students to do research into the topic of fallacies. If you combine this chapter with the one on evidence, you could also make this a disciplines-based activity because fallacies differ from field to field.

It's important to note that fallacies are not always mortal errors in argument. They represent reasoning that is in *some way* faulty or that is likely to be rejected by a *particular* audience. Arguments that one audience might accept could be rejected by another audience that considers the reasoning fallacious. We've given some examples of this problem in the text, but you could find many more in the pages of your local newspaper or even in your students' papers.

Not Just Words

This particular exercise is likely to provoke a spirited response from students, most of whom have seen years and years of warnings against drugs and alcohol. To extend the exercise, ask students to examine the archives at www.adcouncil.org and choose what they think are the most effective public service advertisements. You might also ask them to create their own posters or presentations that they think would be more effective than what they've seen in the past.

Respond

1. The following list of political slogans or phrases may be examples of logical fallacies. Discuss each item to determine what you may know about the slogan. Then decide which, if any, fallacy might be used to describe it.
   - "Leave no child behind." (George Bush policy and slogan) **[sentimental appeal]**
   - "It's the economy, stupid." (sign on the wall at Bill Clinton's campaign headquarters) **[bandwagon appeal; possibly faulty causality]**
   - "Nixon's the one." (campaign slogan) **[begging the question; equivocation]**
   - "Remember the Alamo." (battle cry) **[possibly a *non sequitur* or faulty causality]**
   - "Make love, not war." (antiwar slogan during the Vietnam War) **[either/or; dogmatism]**
   - "A chicken in every pot." (campaign slogan) **[possibly a *non sequitur* or faulty causality]**
   - "No taxation without representation." (American colonial slogan) **[possibly a *non sequitur*; either/or]**
   - "Loose lips sink ships." (slogan from World War II) **[possibly a *non sequitur* or faulty causality]**
   - "Guns don't kill, people do." (NRA slogan) **[faulty causality]**
   - "If you can't stand the heat, get out of the kitchen." (attributed to Harry S. Truman) **[either/or]**
   - "We are the ones we've been waiting for. We are the change that we seek." (Obama campaign statement) **[possibly false authority or a bandwagon appeal]**

2–5. Your students might really enjoy exercise 2 if you encourage them to write extreme examples of the fallacies. It's a little like asking them to engage in a liars' contest, and students might enjoy reading their results aloud. Exercises 3 and 4 ask students to find fallacies in other texts. These exercises might prove to be difficult, but that difficulty will help students understand that many so-called fallacies are audience-specific. Exercise 5, which asks students to see how other writers read fallacies, might also reinforce the slipperiness of calling an argument fallacious.

CHAPTER 18

Intellectual Property, Academic Integrity, and Avoiding Plagiarism

First-year writers have probably received some instruction in the concerns of intellectual property, and they're probably aware of the debates around movie and music piracy. They likely have heard of plagiarism in high school, have been taught not to copy others' work, and understand that plagiarizing is a form of cheating. But plagiarism is only a small part of the intellectual-property debate, and its parameters are far from well defined. You can help your students learn to use sources responsibly if you show them the range of activities that could reasonably constitute plagiarism, from simple copying of text without quotation or attribution to including images on a Web site that the student did not create. Students need to learn that intellectual property can be as jealously guarded as material property, if not more so: material goods can usually be replaced, but intellectual work is not easy to return.

The first-year writing class is usually the place where students learn to respect intellectual property rights and where they struggle with the boundaries of appropriate attribution. As the teacher, you can decide how strict to be with violations of intellectual property. Our experience has been that, for the most part, students do not intend to cheat or to copy without attribution. In most cases, they have simply misunderstood the rules of attribution or have not thought carefully enough about their use of sources. If you use a process model in your course, you could encourage these students to write another draft, this time with appropriate use of sources. Not all incidents of plagiarism are simply well-intentioned mistakes, but we argue for a generous conception of teaching in the first-year course. If students continue to violate the boundaries of intellectual property after you've been thorough in your instruction, you should take appropriate action.

Not Just Words

Intellectual property can be a hot-button issue with many students because of the lawsuits brought against young people who have downloaded music and video from the Web, but this essential chapter may not be the most exciting reading for students. Fortunately, this is an entertaining exercise that asks students to produce their own parody. Ask students to review "Using Humor" on pp. 48–50 before they create their parody.

Respond

1–4. The exercises for this chapter focus mainly on the differences among the various forms of intellectual-property protection. You could combine these exercises with a discussion of the protections available to people in different academic fields. For example, how do scientists in college biology departments protect their work? What about historians? How does each person build on previous work in the field without "copying"? Exercise 4 should be particularly useful for illustrating that intellectual property is as important an issue outside the classroom as it is inside it.

CHAPTER 19

Evaluating and Using Sources

Many of our comments from Chapter 18 apply here, too: students rarely *try* to cheat or get away with misusing intellectual property. You will serve your students—and the purposes of the first-year writing course—if you consider most problems with attribution to be mistakes rather than cheating attempts: students simply don't understand the parameters of responsible use. Many students have to struggle to write their own thoughts and arguments; integrating others' ideas is a real challenge.

Assessing sources can also be a challenge for students. Because the Internet makes finding material so easy, some students will be satisfied with the thousands of hits they get on any search. You will have to teach your students to be very critical of Internet sources: for example, a personal homepage on legalizing marijuana is significantly less credible than refereed research on hemp agriculture, but your students might not see the difference. The chapter includes a list of questions students can ask to determine the quality of any source, electronic or not.

Not Just Words

Students are frequently skeptical of media sources, and this exercise might help them think carefully about the many layers involved in a media presentation. Press them to articulate what makes a source reliable: What level of accuracy should we be able to expect from journalists? What kinds of mistakes are forgivable? What kind of correction can excuse an error? How much are we responsible for knowing when we consume media?

Respond

1–3. The exercises focus largely on the problems of authority and credibility in assessing sources. You could ask students to compile a "first-pass" bibliography on a given topic and then to make a second pass, evaluating the sources for inclusion in a shorter list.

The chapter describes the differences among quotations, paraphrases, and summaries, and the first exercise helps them practice recognizing these different forms of using research. Students will probably benefit from practicing these techniques throughout the course, though the more context you can give them, the better. Rather than ask for summaries or paraphrases that are unrelated to students' long writing assignments, suggest that students write paraphrases or summaries in preparation for their other work. Carefully integrate the techniques into the larger concerns of the course. Remind students to take special care when researching online, as it's easy to surf through multiple sources without taking thorough notes about where you've been and when you were there.

CHAPTER 20

Documenting Sources

Most of this chapter is concerned with the technical details of the MLA and APA citation systems, not with the way citation and documentation constitute a form of argument. The details are not hard to master, but they are complicated and reward careful attention. Our experience has been that first-year students will make up their own citation systems—with some mix of dates, names, and titles, rarely consistent—unless they are asked to follow MLA or APA guidelines carefully. Remind them that citation is largely a mechanical skill and that they need to use the models to learn how to format citations and bibliographies appropriately. Not many students need to memorize a citation system, and no one needs to memorize every possibility; they simply need to get comfortable with looking up the formatting and applying it correctly.

Not Just Words

This exercise calls attention to the appearance of citations and how Web sites have chosen a form of documentation that helps to emphasize readability, as the links do not distract much from the text. However, links also hide some of the information that citations usually provide, as a reader may not be able to figure out what site the link connects to. Further, the chances for losing an audience completely are high—readers may click on a link and never return to the original article.

If you're teaching MLA format, you might talk about how MLA style attempts to minimize distractions to the reader by encouraging researchers to include authors' names in the text of the paper rather than just in the parenthetical citation and by placing most parenthetical citations at the ends of sentences.

Part of the goal of teaching citation, after all, is teaching students that a documentation style is not just a random collection of rules but a system designed to make intellectual inquiry open and honest.

Respond

1. This exercise asks students to identify the ways certain citation systems make arguments in themselves. Draw your students' attention to the relative placements of author, date of publication, and title in MLA and APA styles. You could ask your students to develop alternative citation styles that reflect some other values or priorities: How would they cite sources if they were concerned primarily with the author's credibility? Would book sales ever be an appropriate measure to cite in a bibliography?
2. This exercise allows students to practice citing works (e.g., songs) that they might be surprised to learn are covered by MLA and APA. This exercise should be fairly quick and simple for students, but make sure that they take the time to get their citations correct. Students must pay close attention to details to make sure they cite correctly.

CHAPTER 21

How Does Popular Culture Stereotype *You*?

Through the media—newspapers, magazines, radio, television, films, and the Internet—we regularly encounter stereotypes of various groups in our society. Whether based on some measure of reality or not, these stereotypes become part of our cultural folklore, and many people's perceptions of ethnic and social groups are based solely on representations they see in the media. How do we know when a representation will be accepted as tongue-in-cheek, ironic, or offensive, or even perceived as true?

- Do the media represent people as ideal types—that is, as we wish we were or as others (marketers? groups with various kinds of social power?) wish we were? If so, to what extent are these practices harmful? To whom? Why?
- Do the media represent some segments of the population in terms of ideal types and other segments in terms of stereotypes? If so, to what extent are these practices damaging? To whom? Why?
- When do the media influence us directly? When are they mediated in some way—that is, linked to complex changes that, in turn, influence attitudes or behaviors?

Sam Dillon *Evictions at Sorority Raise Issue of Bias* pp. 603–6

1. What examples of stereotyping do you find in this article? Who is being stereotyped? What or who, do you believe, are the sources of the stereotypes?

   The women who were evicted from the house may have been stereotyped as uncool or "not sorority material." The description of the women from Indiana University as "plas-

tic women" might serve as an example of a stereotype of those involved in Greek life.

What evidence is there in the article of people who are criticizing or contesting stereotypes? Who are they, and how are they calling stereotypes into question?

The women who are complaining about being moved to alumna status are criticizing and contesting stereotypes by suggesting that what matters in a good sorority is a diversity of women, not a certain look or social status.

2. Paragraphs 13–14 provide historical background about Delta Zeta sorority on the DePauw campus. Is this information necessary to the article? If so, how? If not, why not? What is the relationship between paragraphs 13–14 and paragraphs 15–16? What is the role of these two latter paragraphs in the article?

   Paragraphs 13 and 14 suggest a history of discrimination in this particular sorority, especially on the part of the national office. The information is not strictly necessary and may be read as either useful background or an unfair reminder of a distant past. Paragraphs 15 and 16 suggest some differences between the local chapter and the national office over the past few years, as these paragraphs suggest that the local chapter has a recent history of being inclusive.

3. In printed newspapers, corrections appear several days after the original article is printed, but someone doing research might well not notice them. In contrast, a correction posted on an electronic source will always be available to future readers. In some cases, the correction is incorporated into the original article rather than being noted separately at the end of the article. The correction that appears at the end of this article reminds us that even award-winning journalists sometimes make errors. How serious, in your opinion, was the error in Dillon's original article? Does this correction influence how you read or evaluate the article? Does it influence how you evaluate the ethos of the writer? (For a discussion of ethos, see Chapter 3.)

   Answers will vary.

4–5. Writing assignments

Classroom Exercise: focus on the world

If your school has Greek organizations, what stereotypes do you see for individual organizations or for Greek life as a whole? Think about other student organizations on your campus—sports teams, religious groups, minority organizations, or majors from a particular school or department. Do you think that your campus stereotypes individuals? Can you make an argument about how stereotypes might be useful or even helpful on a college campus? Can you offer evidence that stereotyping causes real harm to individuals?

Ellen Goodman *The Culture of Thin Bites Fiji* pp. 608–9

1. What is Goodman's argument?

   She argues that popular culture teaches girls and women to hate and harm themselves.

   How does she build it around Becker's study while not limiting herself to that evidence alone? (Consider, especially, paragraphs 15–17.)

   She does it by framing Becker's study within her own prose. She opens with an invitation to her readers to imagine a situation that sets up the background for describing Becker's research. She concludes by pulling back and adding her own commentary and recontextualizing the discussion in terms of the Columbine school killings.

2. What knowledge of popular American culture does Goodman assume that her *Boston Globe* audience has?

   She expects them to have familiarity with popular TV shows, knowledge of the high incidence of eating disorders among young women, and awareness of incidents of killings in schools by young male students.

   How does she use allusions to American TV programs to build her argument? Note, for example, that she sometimes uses such allusions as conversational asides—"All that and these islanders didn't even get *Ally McBeal*," and "At this rate, we owe the islanders at least one year of the ample lawyer Camryn Manheim in *The Practice* for free"—to establish her ethos. (For a discussion of ethos, see Chapter 3.)

Answers will vary. One strong possibility is that Goodman invokes shared knowledge to establish credibility with her audience and develop her ethos as someone in touch with popular culture.

In what other ways do allusions to TV programs contribute to Goodman's argument?

They provide specific evidence of the material viewed by Fijians.

Do you understand her allusions to 1995's TV programs or popular culture? If not, how are you in the same situation as the islanders? If you do understand, offer to explain the allusions to your classmates who don't.

Answers will vary.

3. At least by implication, if not in fact, Goodman makes a causal argument about the entertainment industry, women's body image, and the consequences of such an image. What sort of causal argument does she set up? (For a discussion of causal arguments, see Chapter 11.)

   She uses Anne Becker's research about teens in Fiji to argue about the effects of the entertainment industry on women's body image: teenage girls who watch popular American television shows develop a skewed image of the ideal female body size and shape.

   How effective do you find it? Why?

   Answers will vary.

4. Writing assignment

Classroom Exercise: focus on the world

Goodman's conclusion links eating disorders and recent school killings, stating that the media heavily influence adolescents to be destructive. How persuasive is this link? How similar are the two types of destructive behavior that Goodman cites—the destruction of others committed by certain boys and the self-destruction committed by certain girls? How is the role of the media similar in the two types of destruction? How is it different?

Anne E. Becker *Abstract, Discussion, and Conclusions of Television, Disordered Eating, and Young Women in Fiji: Negotiating Body Image and Identity during Rapid Social Change* pp. 611–19

1. How does Becker link exposure to Western media to the changing notions young Fijian women have of their own bodies?

   The author interviewed young women in a rural town of Fiji three years after the introduction of television to the community. The social interviews focused on body image, and the researcher also analyzed the girls' references to media images.

   Why does Becker claim these women now want to be thin? How are these changes linked to other social changes occurring in Fiji, to adolescence, and to gender, especially in small-scale societies?

   Young women's focus has shifted from their communities' traditional values to the Western value of consumerism. They identify with television characters and celebrity lifestyles, and they equate too much weight with laziness and thinness with success. Fiji is also facing economic and social changes as it looks out onto a globalizing world. Young women are especially susceptible to these outside media forces in a climate of rapid social change when they are searching for role models. Women in general must consider self-presentation for social status in an environment where merit is ascribed, not achieved.

2. As Becker notes, she relies on qualitative data—specifically interview data—to support her arguments. Why are such data especially appropriate, given her goals of understanding the changing social meanings of body image for young Fijian women as part of other rapid social changes taking place in Fiji? (For a discussion of firsthand evidence, see Chapter 16.)

   Interview data are firsthand evidence that may not be available through observations or even questionnaires. The perspective of a person involved in a specific situation is invaluable, especially in a changing social atmosphere where other types of evidence may be difficult to collect.

3. Throughout the Discussion and Conclusions sections, Becker repeatedly qualifies her arguments to discourage readers from extending them further than she believes her data warrant. Find two cases where she does so, and explain in the specific ways that she reminds readers of the limits of her claims. (For a discussion on qualifying claims and arguments, see Chapter 7.)

   Answers will vary, but some examples include her use of "minimally" and "quite possibly." When Becker tells us that "Minimally . . . narrative data reflect a shift in fashion," she lets the reader know that her data report at least this fact and might have further implications. Her use of a qualifier in "Quite possibly . . . disordered eating may also be a symbolic embodiment of the anxiety and conflict the youth experience" suggests that the eating behavior of women is more complicated than a reaction to seeing beautiful people on television.

4. These excerpts from Becker's article represent research writing for an academic audience. What functions does each of the reprinted sections serve for the article's readers, and why is each located where it is? Why, for example, is an abstract placed at the beginning of an article? Why are keywords a valuable part of an abstract?

   The delineated sections of the article give structure to the paper and create focal points for different information about the study. The abstract tells us what to expect from the paper as a whole, so it comes first. The discussion analyzes the data that have been presented. The conclusions draw the various points together with some implications for further research or action. The keywords present the main themes of the paper so that the reader can judge the relevance of the article to the information that they seek.

5. Writing assignment

Classroom Exercise: focus on the argument

Becker reports that beauty standards are changing in Fiji due to the influx of Western ideals, specifically television images of slender women. Consider your response to this research. Would you have imagined that television could have such an effect in a culture with a long history of appreciating full-figured women? Is the problem that women want to be thin, or is their dangerous manner of losing weight the issue? Should one or both issues be addressed? Should young Fijian women be encouraged to return to their traditional beauty ideals? Using Becker's article as your source material, hold a debate or roundtable discussion in your class.

Making a Visual Argument

KennethCole.com *We All Walk in Different Shoes* pp. 621–22

1. What is your initial response to this ad? How does it fit into the series in which it appears, as described in the headnote to this selection?

   Answers will vary.

   How have the designers of the ads played with stereotypes?

   Most of these models defy our expectations: the beautiful woman who appears first is transgender; the bald woman is presented as a sex symbol; the African American model is albino and so does not appear as we expect African Americans to appear; we do not expect Hasidic Jews to be reggae artists or reggae artists to be Hasidic Jews; we do not expect punk rockers to be evangelists or evangelists to be punk rockers.

   How does the choice of individuals who are included (none is a professional model) further the claim that "We all walk in different shoes"?

   Cole chooses models who have identities that we don't expect, and the ads encourage us to think about what life would be like for someone who has faced difficult experiences (e.g., ovarian cancer) or potentially experienced alienation from two communities (e.g., a punk evangelist is likely to be at odds with other punks and with other evangelicals).

2. Advertising focuses heavily on emotional arguments, although it often presents ethical and logical arguments as well. Where do you find evidence of each in this ad?

   Answers will vary. Some possibilities follow: Emotional arguments are presented when the ad encourages our

sympathy for the suffering that this model may have endured, and we might also see a humorous appeal in the way that Cole defies our expectations of who can be a model. One logical appeal comes in the title "We all walk in different shoes," which invites us to think about the figurative meaning of the phrase and the diversity of experience among all of us

3. Writing assignment

Classroom Exercise: focus on the argument

You have undoubtedly heard that physical appearance is increasingly important in the United States and elsewhere. Do you agree with this observation? Using only your own personal experiences as evidence—not what you've read or what your friends or relatives have related to you—support or refute the claim that appearance has, in your lifetime, become more important as a measure of a person's worth. (We imagine that many students will find it difficult to avoid citing what they've read or heard from others. This exercise is intended to make students aware of the extent to which their beliefs are shaped by the experiences of others and also to enhance their ability to assess different types of evidence.)

Barbara Munson *Common Themes and Questions about the Use of "Indian" Logos* pp. 624–30

1. What's Munson's argument? Why is it stated where and as it is? How might her purpose in writing have led her to present her material in this way?

   Munson's argument, which opens the selection, is that the use of Indian logos promotes racism. Stating this thesis succinctly at the beginning of the manifesto leaves readers with no question about what they can expect as they read.

   Would the selection have been more or less effective if she'd formatted her argument as a "regular" essay, consisting of an introduction that leads to her thesis statement, several paragraphs of a body, and a conclusion? Why?

   The presentation of point and counterpoint guides the readers through the piece and addresses the most common defenses of the use of Indian logos. This organization high-

lights each of the points that Munson refutes and speaks to the reader in a way that a traditional essay might not.

2. Examine the "common questions and statements" to which Munson replies and try to determine why she arranged them in this order. Would her argument be strengthened or weakened if these paragraphs were in a different order?

   The organization of the topics adds to the strength of the argument. Munson moves from the most obvious questions to the more difficult questions that people raise about the issue. Ending with a question and response about why schools are reluctant to change their Indian logos shows that Munson is aware of the complicated nature of the debate.

   Are there advantages and disadvantages to such implicit organization of an argument?

   The advantage to such organization is a smooth flow of ideas throughout the piece. A disadvantage is that the thesis and supports are not presented concisely but rather are restated at different times throughout the article.

3. How would you characterize Munson's tone in this selection? Her ethos? What evidence would you cite for your conclusions? How do her tone and ethos contribute to or detract from her argument?

   Answers will vary. Some might say that Munson's tone is serious, controlled, and evenhanded and that this tone contributes to an ethos of knowledge and experience, which adds to her argument by creating credibility. Others might find her unwilling to compromise and believe that she is overly certain that she is right, thus detracting from her ethos. Whatever students believe about her tone, push them to provide evidence for their conclusions.

   Would you characterize this argument as Rogerian? (For a discussion of Rogerian argumentation, see Chapter 1.) Why or why not?

   Answers will vary, but we feel that her argument is not Rogerian. The first paragraph of the essay does not attempt to build an argument out of common ground; Munson presents a thesis that Native American mascots and logos do

harm and does not waver or find much good in opposing arguments.

4. One of Munson's concerns is the influence of "Indian" logos on children, both Native American and non-Indian. Do you agree with her argument? Why or why not?

   Answers will vary.

   How does her mention of children early in the argument add to the weight or gravity of her topic as she defines it?

   She argues that racism is persistent. Exposing children—the next generation—to racist views in school negatively affects the future.

5. Although American Indian logos, names, mascots, and symbols show up in many places in popular culture, Munson is concerned specifically with athletics and sports events. Why?

   Munson states that the use of Indian logos as part of another culture's games is particularly insulting. Further, in American culture athletics are frequently tied to schools, and for schools to be participating in institutional racism is especially egregious for Munson. Additionally, Indian students face racism and non-Indian students see or participate in racist acts whenever an Indian mascot is displayed. This activity divorces the Indian people from the symbols of their heritage.

   In what sense does her article demonstrate that these logos, names, mascots, and symbols have become part of larger political debates? (For a discussion of evaluative arguments, see Chapter 10.)

   She describes objections to her position such as claims that the debate about Indian logos is just an extension of political correctness or minority complaining.

6. Writing assignment

Classroom Exercise: focus on the argument

Does your university or college use an Indian logo or another ethnic logo? How about students' favorite professional teams? How do students feel about changing these names and mascots? Do they have suggestions of other names and images that satisfactorily represent the spirit of the school? Does changing the mascot somehow break the chain of tradition? Does it change the ethos of the institution? Do people in the community in which the students are studying think that the change would be worth the effort?

Joe Lapointe *Bonding over a Mascot* pp. 632–34

1. The selection offers some insights into how and why Florida State University has been able to retain its mascot, the Seminole, despite the 2005 NCAA rules. Based on this article, how and why has the discussion at Florida State moved past an argument over stereotypes?

   The discussion has moved past an argument about stereotypes because the Seminole Tribe of Florida has been involved in decisions about the use of the mascot.

   What problems has bonding over the mascot solved for the various parties involved?

   The university now does not face NCAA sanctions, and the Seminole Tribe does not feel demeaned by the use of the mascot.

   Which problems has it not solved?

   Some people still disapprove of some of the stereotypical Indian trappings such as the tomahawk chop or the traditional FSU cheer. Further, the bonding over this mascot does not easily apply to how other schools use Native American figures as mascots.

2. This article carries the title "Bonding over a Mascot." (As you may be aware, journalists rarely, if ever, title their own articles.) We might also read the article as an analysis of the ways in which Florida State and the Seminole Tribe have bonded against the NCAA. What are the advantages for each group of bonding against the NCAA over the mascot?

   The school retains the ability to use their traditional mascot and, at least somewhat, argues that they've been more sensitive to the Seminole Tribe than the NCAA, which lumped together all uses of Native American mascots. The Seminole

Tribe has some control over how the image of the Seminole appears.

How has such cooperation worked, at least in the eyes of some, to reduce demeaning stereotypes?

Input into the image of the Seminole means that some of the more offensive images, such as Sammy Seminole, can be phased out, while aspects of Seminole heritage that the Tribe hopes to celebrate, such as never surrendering to the U.S. government, can be highlighted.

3. Like most writers, Lapointe relies on ethical appeals in constructing his argument—his own ethos and the ethos of those he quotes. Whom does he choose to quote in this article?

   Lapointe quotes a student with Seminole heritage; leaders of the Seminole Tribe of Florida, Florida State University, and the NCAA; two history professors from FSU; and a leader of the Florida Governor's Council on Indian Affairs.

   How does the identity of these individuals—who they are or the role that they play—influence their credibility with you as a reader?

   Answers will vary.

   How would the article have been different if Lapointe had begun it by focusing on Seminole students who were unhappy with their tribe's decision?

   Answers will vary. One possibility: if Lapointe had begun with Seminole students unhappy with their tribe's decision, we might be more inclined to see the agreement to use the mascot as a deal made by people in power who weren't paying attention to the desires of individual tribe members. We might then be more inclined to find the mascot offensive.

4. How might Barbara Munson, author of the previous selection, "Common Themes and Questions about the Use of 'Indian' Logos," respond to Toni Sanchez's position as expressed in this article? Why?

   Munson would likely argue that the use of the Seminole mascot does not honor the Seminoles but places Seminole culture in the past and highlights only the warrior aspect of

the Seminole Tribe, which recalls only a tragic era of Seminole history.

5. Writing assignment

Classroom Exercise: focus on rhetoric

Question 3 asks students to think about ethos in this article, and that topic is worth spending some time discussing in class. Who has the right to talk about issues of minority representation? Who has the right to decide whether a team's mascot is appropriate? You might have students research the fact that Florida State President T. K. Wetherell submitted a letter of resignation pending the hiring of a successor in the summer of 2009. After reading his letter of resignation, what did they think of his ethos? Do students feel that they would trust Wetherell or Barbara Munson, author of the previous selection, "Common Themes and Questions about the Use of 'Indian' Logos," more on questions about appropriate school mascots? Or to take the discussion away from mascots: What place do nonminorities have in discussions of how minorities are represented?

Stuart Elliott *Uncle Ben, Board Chairman* pp. 636–39

1. Are you convinced? How successful has Mars been in reclaiming the image of Uncle Ben? To what extent do you find that your responses to Mars's efforts are based on fact and reason? On your emotional response? On your willingness to trust the arguments made by Mars about why it is doing what it has done? Once you have responded to this question, visit the Uncle Ben's Web site (http://unclebens.com) and see whether your response changes.

   Answers will vary; as always, the key is to make sure that students articulate why they have the reactions that they do—what kinds of rhetorical situations are they entering?

2. Increasingly, public figures, especially women in the world of entertainment, are referred to by their first names alone (such is the case with Oprah Winfrey, Martha Stewart, Tyra Banks, Madonna Ciccone, and the late Diana, Princess of Wales). Why is the issue of Uncle Ben's lack of a last name an important one for many people?

   People without last names may seem to be trademarks or marketing vehicles or something other than real people.

How does an understanding of the history of the African American experience help account for this concern?

One tactic for dehumanizing slaves was to refuse to call them by their original names and assign them new ones. Also, as the article points out, white southerners often used the titles "aunt" and "uncle" because they refused to refer to African Americans as "mister" or "miss," as those words were too respectful.

3. Paragraph 13 of this selection explains that many early ad characters fell into disuse and those that were retained were rendered silent, "removed from ads and reduced to staring mutely from packages." Why do you imagine that these characters were no longer allowed to speak? In other words, in what ways can an ad character's speech contribute to, encourage, or call into question negative stereotypes?

Answers will vary, but ad characters with a heavy dialect or who sound unintelligent could clearly reinforce negative stereotypes.

4–5. Writing assignments

Classroom Exercise: focus on the world

Do students think about ad characters that companies create? Ask the class to brainstorm a list of fictional ad characters who are similar in their representation of a company to Uncle Ben (though you might encourage them to think not only of people—the Geico gecko, for example, could be included). Do they find that these characters have a trustworthy ethos? Are there some that they find objectionable? Do they find that ad characters are something that they even respond to? A discussion about ad characters can be productive for thinking about ethos, as companies who use these characters are only creating an ethos and not dealing with real human beings. Ask students to compare different ad characters and evaluate the appropriateness of the ethos that each company has created.

Charles A. Riley II *Disability and the Media: Prescriptions for Change* pp. 641–50

1. In what ways does Riley contend that the media and popular culture wrongly stereotype people with disabilities?

Riley contends that the media patronize people with disabilities by treating their disability as the only significant aspect of their identity and by focusing on the process of overcoming the disability to fit into mainstream society as the most significant achievement in their lives.

What negative consequences follow from this stereotyping for such people? For those who do not have disabilities? Why?

These stereotypes treat the disabled as less than fully human and in some situations may make their suffering seem almost desirable. Audiences often have their sympathies manipulated and misunderstand the nature of the disability. Audiences also sometimes develop a sense of superiority since they are not disabled.

2. How convincingly has Riley defined a problem or need, which is the first step in a proposal argument? (For a discussion of proposal arguments, see Chapter 12.)

   Answers will vary.

3. What is your response to "Appendix A: Guidelines for Portraying People with Disabilities in the Media"? Are you familiar with the practices that these guidelines seek to prevent? Do you find the guidelines useful or necessary? Why or why not? What justification might be offered for why specific guidelines are important?

   Answers will vary; especially if students think that Riley is obviously right or obviously wrong, press them to use reasons and warrants to explain their thinking.

4–5. Writing assignments

Classroom Exercise: focus on the argument

Anyone who has watched sports on television, and especially the Olympics, has seen stories about how athletes have overcome personal tragedies or grave health concerns. Do stories of overcoming adversity consistently reduce the subjects of these stories to plot elements instead of real people? What are the dangers of reducing people to what Riley calls "allegorical flatness"? Can students offer an argument defending stories of adversity, even those that rely on traditional storylines?

Wrap-up Exercises for "How Does Popular Culture Stereotype *You*?"

The following questions invite students to consider themes from the readings in this cluster. They can be used for extended projects as well as in-class essay questions.

1. Write a personal response to one or both of the topics of the two clusters in this chapter: representations of the body or stereotypes of groups. In your response, detail your understanding of the impact of images in the media on your own life. Do you see yourself and people like you (in any sort of way) represented in the media? If you do, where? How often? In what sorts of roles or situations? What are the consequences of these facts for you? For those like you? For those who are not like you? If you do not see yourself or others like you (in any sort of way) represented in the media, what are the consequences of that fact for you? For others like you? For those who are not like you?

2. This chapter explores how the media stereotype certain categories of Americans, especially minorities, and in most cases the readings suggest that stereotypes present a danger to individuals, to a group, or to the culture. Write an essay in which you examine the potential consequences of media stereotypes for society as a whole or for a particular group or person. Note that you might wish to argue that there are no negative consequences of media stereotypes or that, if there are, we should not be concerned with them. Your essay will likely be most successful if you are careful to qualify your claims and to cite specific evidence, rather than dealing in vague generalities.

How Many Friends Have You Made Today?

The readings in this chapter consider social network sites—sites that likely play a large role in the lives of many of our students—from academic and professional angles. The stases of cause and evaluation are especially important in this chapter as writers study the effects of this new technology and try to determine if, overall, social network sites are positive or negative influences in our lives.

The researchers quoted in this chapter seem to find mostly positive benefits to the online activities of young people, but plenty of warnings about the dangers of the Internet pepper this chapter. It's likely that this chapter will help students think more critically and consciously about a part of their life that, for many of them, consumes many hours each day, so the first question at the end of this chapter asks students to make sense of their own experience with social network sites in light of what they read here. Some of the questions that are central to the readings of this chapter follow.

- How does participation in social network sites and other online activities shape or even create our identity?
- How can we manage and control our online lives to preserve our safety and the integrity of our identity?
- How do we make sense of the relationships that we forge online? What responsibilities do we have to others and to ourselves when we are online?

danah m. boyd and Nicole B. Ellison *Social Network Sites: Definition, History, and Scholarship* pp. 653–67

1. How much of the information in this selection is new to you? Were you aware of any, some, most, or all of the developments that boyd and Ellison discuss?

Answers will vary.

Why is it useful for researchers to write articles that lay out criteria for defining a social phenomenon and trace its history?

The study might be considered useful because it can help us understand our relationship with a new technology and how that technology changes our lives.

2. Evaluate the section of the article entitled "Social Network Sites: A Definition" as an argument of definition. What kind(s) of definition do the authors offer?

   A formal definition, perhaps also definitions by example.

   Why do they prefer the term "social network site" to "social networking site" (paragraph 6)?

   The authors prefer the word "network" because it describes the web of interaction that participants join; "networking" emphasizes the act of initiating new contacts, but most participants are communicating with people they already know.

   How persuasive are their arguments for this choice? How effective is their definition of this category of Web sites? (For a discussion of arguments of definition, see Chapter 9.)

   Answers will vary.

3. Evaluate the section of the article entitled "A History of Social Network Sites" as a factual argument. Why does the subsection "The Early Years" begin with the statement, "According to the definition above,. . ." (paragraph 16)? In other words, why did the authors provide a definitional argument before an argument of fact about the history of social network sites?

   The authors need to establish the definition for the phenomenon because otherwise they can't explain a history of the phenomenon—they have to set out the criteria so that they have a starting point and can explain how things have changed.

   What sorts of evidence do the authors cite in constructing this argument?

   They cite personal communication and news articles from cNet and Inc. magazine.

Why do they frequently cite personal communications? (For a discussion of arguments of fact, see Chapter 8.)

The personal communications come from people who worked for or developed the SNSs, so they are authoritative sources. Also, because the SNSs are recent phenomena, there is not a developed body of published scholarship on the topic.

4. What role(s) does Figure 1 play in the authors' argument?

   Figure 1 supports the idea that an SNS can attract a diverse audience with diverse interests and also highlights the idea that many people on an SNS are looking to connect with people who share their interests (perhaps to extend a social network already in existence).

   Would the article have been weaker without it? Why or why not? (For a discussion of visual arguments, see Chapter 14.)

   Answers will vary.

5. Writing assignment

Classroom Exercise: focus on the world

Beginning with the distinction between "social networking sites" and "social network sites" and what that difference implies about how people use these sites, interview a friend who participates in an SNS and write an argument about how social network sites have played a role in your friend's life. Think carefully about which stasis you mean to emphasize: are you writing a causal argument? evaluating your friend's experience? Do you want to make a proposal about how your friend could use an SNS more effectively or about how your friend spends too much time online? Review Chapter 16 for more information on interviewing.

Office of the Privacy Commissioner of Canada *A Friend of a Friend of a Friend Knows You're on Vacation* pp. 669–71

1. What are the purposes of and occasions for these arguments?

   An argument to inform in a time of perceived threat.

How would you characterize these arguments in terms of stasis theory? (For a discussion of the purposes of and occasions for arguments as well as stasis theory, see Chapter 1.)

Definition: Defines SNSs as profit-seeking operations.
Causal: Asks questions about potentially negative effects of sharing data.
Proposal: Encourages us to think more carefully about how we handle our personal information.

How effective are these arguments? Why?

Answers will vary.

2. Focus on the written and read-aloud versions of the transcript of the YouTube video. How effective is the reader of the transcript in presenting the argument that he is reading? How does he use intonation rhetorically as he performs the transcript? In what ways does the video represent an argument to be heard? (For a discussion of presenting arguments, see Chapter 15.)

   Answers will vary. We find the rhetorical performance to be a bit machinelike, as though he were reminding us of the threat of a computer that followed its own agenda (as in the film *2001: A Space Odyssey*). We think that menacing tone is an intentional feature of the video, thus establishing this video as an argument to be heard.

3. Focus on the visual information that is presented in the video. What information and what kinds of information are presented? You might want to make a list of all of the visual images that are presented in the video and then categorize these images according to type and function.

   The video begins with pictures that look like typical user-profile pictures plus a few photographs of technology; then it primarily relies on graphic representations of how users and data interconnect, along with text of what information these sites gather and some of their legal language.

   How relevant or necessary is this information to the overall argument made by the video? (For a discussion of visual arguments, see Chapter 14.)

   Answers will vary, but the graphs seem important to dis-

playing how individuals are not of primary importance because trends and patterns are what the sites pay attention to.

4. Writing assignment

Classroom Exercise: focus on the argument

How seriously do students take this warning? Given that we take risks in our lives every day—driving, for example, can be an extremely risky activity—how do we weigh the risks associated with sharing personal information online? Do students believe that their peers would take notice of this argument? Ask students to prepare a presentation, a video, or a short paper that would serve as a more effective warning for their peers about the risks of social network sites.

Heather Havenstein *One in Five Employers Uses Social Networks in Hiring Process* pp. 673–74

1. Statistics play an important role in Havenstein's argument. How would the article be different if she had not used statistics? How effective would it be? Why? (To think about this question, you might mentally remove the statistics in the list in paragraph 4 while substituting more general statements for statistical claims in the text so that "one in five" in the first paragraph becomes "a few.")

   Answers may vary, but the argument seems largely built on statistics. It would not be nearly as persuasive if they were absent because the information might seem vague.

2. Havenstein's article is brief and to the point. Why do you think that brevity and directness characterize much of the writing for *Computerworld* and other sources of information about technology on the Internet?

   Some possible answers include because of the speed with which we read on the Internet (many people tend to skim more when reading online material, and *Computerworld* is an online resource), the ease with which we can click to new sites, and the sheer mass of information available.

3. Analyze Havenstein's article as a proposal argument. What problem is addressed?

Job seekers are often unaware that potential employers use social network sites in hiring decisions.

The claim?

Many hiring managers choose not to hire potential employees based on information found on social network sites.

The proposal? (For a discussion of proposal arguments, see Chapter 12.)

Job seekers should carefully control their self-presentation on social network sites.

4. In many ways, Havenstein's article can be seen as a logical follow-up to the previous selection, "A Friend of a Friend of a Friend Knows You're on Vacation." It provides a case study on issues of privacy and social network sites, one dealing with the specific situation of job seekers. Based on the information in the previous selection or your own experience, how likely is it that following the suggestions of CareerBuilder will remove all evidence of potentially objectionable behavior from a social network site?

   Answers will vary, but it seems unlikely that objectionable information will be removed given that our friends and acquaintances might post information about us and that all posted information becomes property of the SNS.

5–6. Writing assignments

Classroom Exercise: focus on rhetoric

Ask students to examine their own personal presentation on a social network site, if applicable. Then ask them what ethos they would like to present to a potential employer and what changes they would make to their own profile to create that ethos. Be sure that students are not just thinking about a generic employer but one for whom they would actually like to work, so that they develop the skill of thinking critically about an intended audience. If students do not already have an online profile, ask them to think about what they would include if they were to construct one. If time allows, have the students trade descriptions of their profiles or take a look at their current online profiles and discuss what kind of ethos is being created.

Tamar Lewin *Study Finds Teenagers' Internet Socializing Isn't Such a Bad Thing* pp. 676–79

1. Who is likely the intended audience for this article? The invoked audience? What evidence can you cite? (For a discussion of audience, see Chapter 1.)

   The intended audience is parents, especially of children old enough to use the Internet. The invoked audience is smaller, "the worried parents" of the first sentence. Students might cite lines such as "in a situation familiar to many parents" as evidence of the audience.

2. Is any of this information news to you?

   Answers will vary.

   Why might it be news to the readers of the *New York Times*?

   Readers of the *New York Times* are likely to be older than the students and so less aware of how SNSs are used; also, older people are usually familiar with fewer young people, so they may fear that their child, who is actually a typical teenager, is an anomaly.

3. How does Lewin move between the findings of the study and interviews with adolescents at a Bronx school?

   Lewin uses a transition phrase ("This is not news to a cluster of Bronx teenagers") that explains how the students were interviewed.

   How does the information gathered from interviews contribute to Lewin's argument?

   Answers will vary, but the interviewed teenagers make heavy use of social network sites and sound entirely typical.

   How would the article be different without this information? (For a discussion of interviewing, see Chapter 16.)

   Answers will vary, but the article would lose the authority that comes from including the firsthand experience that the teenagers detail.

4. How well did you anticipate the topics of the reader comments that were chosen by the *Times*'s editors? To what extent do you agree with the comments?

Answers will vary.

The most developed of the comments was written by Elliot Cole. What is his argument?

Cole essentially argues that new technology is an attempt to revitalize a public space destroyed by previous generations.

What evidence does he give?

His evidence seems mostly to be based on his own experience as a middle- or upper-middle-class suburban American.

In what ways does he believe that the "older generation" is missing the point in many of its complaints about younger people's uses of technology?

He believes that the older generation focuses on surface issues such as spelling rather than the real social needs expressed by participation in social networks.

5. Writing assignment

Classroom Exercise: focus on the argument

Divide the class into groups of two or four and give each group one of the comments from readers. Ask half of each group to write a response to the reader comment, and then have the other half of the group write a response to that comment. The goal of this exercise is for students to pay attention and respond to the rhetorical context that they are entering. Each comment must be clearly based on the previous comment, though they can of course manipulate the conversation to pursue their own claims. Alternatively, have students choose one of the reader comments and either (1) expand the argument into a full essay or (2) refute the argument directly in a full essay.

Mizuko Ito et al. *"Executive Summary," Living and Learning with New Media* pp. 681–84

1. What research questions did the Digital Youth Project seek to answer?

   From paragraph 2: "How are new media being integrated into youth practices and agendas? How do these practices

change the dynamics of youth-adult negotiations over literacy, learning, and authoritative knowledge?"

Based on this summary, what answers have the researchers found?

Youth tend to rely more on self-directed, peer-based learning, which erases more traditional markers of authoritative learning such as age.

2. The summary and accompanying report identify three genres of participation in the new media—hanging out, messing around, and geeking out—each in some sense building on the previous one. (Ethnographers generally label social phenomena with the terms that are used by those they study, so we can assume that the young people in the study used these terms in talking about their experience and those of others.) How does each state represent a deepening and more complex relationship with technology?

   In the move from "friendship-driven practices" ("hanging out") to "interest-driven practices" ("messing around"), young people move into actively seeking new information rather than associating with people they know from other contexts. Additionally, in this move into the second stage young people are likely to develop new media skills that allow them to produce content such as videos or custom games. As they move into the third stage, "self-directed learning" ("geeking out"), the youths produce more content and turn to specialized groups and experts to learn more.

   In what ways does each stage assume different sorts of interpersonal relationships that are mediated by technology, that is, that depend on technology in some way?

   While the first stage depends mostly on relationships from offline lives, the second and third stages depend on relationships with people outside schools and local communities. The more invested young people are in technology, such as when they are geeking out, the more likely that their interpersonal relationships are entirely dependent on having sought out specialized knowledge groups that contain people from around the country and the world.

3. In what ways is the section entitled "Implications for Educators, Parents, and Policymakers" (paragraphs 8–12) a proposal argument?

   This section identifies a problem (adults do not necessarily understand how to manage young people's interactions with new media), suggests actions to take (for example, not putting up barriers for online participation), focuses on the future (how we as a society can benefit from youths' interest in new media), and centers on the audience (this section is written more for parents and educators than for young people).

   In what ways could this section serve as the basis for more specific proposals? (For a discussion of proposal arguments, see Chapter 12.)

   This section offers general guidelines for how parents and educators can think about new media, but it does not explain how we might implement new practices that would take advantage of new media in education.

4. Writing assignment

Classroom Exercise: focus on rhetoric

Summarizing an argument effectively can be a challenging skill for students to develop. Ask students to choose a section of the executive summary and compare that summary to a longer section that appears in the white paper or even the book (both available at http://digitalyouth.ischool.berkeley.edu/report). What kinds of things get left out in an effective summary? Because it is an academic skill that helps students figure out how arguments work, you might also ask them to practice summarizing arguments that appear in these readings.

Mizuko Ito et al. *Geeking Out* pp. 686–97

1. In what ways does the researchers' description of geeking out contrast sharply with stereotypes of geeks in popular culture?

   The description in the article says that geeking out is highly social and engaged, not isolated.

   What kinds of evidence do the researchers provide for their claims?

They rely primarily on interviews and some close study of the products that some members of "geek culture" produce.

How convincing do you find their argument? (For a discussion of evaluating evidence, see Chapter 16.)

Answers will vary.

2. Readers expect arguments that are based on ethnographic methods to be characterized by detailed descriptions of specific cases, events, or situations because such descriptions constitute much of the support for the claims that the arguments make. Choose two such descriptions in this selection that you find especially effective, and explain why you find them successful.

   Answers will vary.

3. Select one of the subsections of this selection (for example, "Specialized Knowledge Networks" or "Interest-Based Communities and Organizations"), and use Toulmin argumentation (see Chapter 7) to analyze its claims. Pay attention to the issue of evidence (as in question 1 above), warrants, backing, and qualifiers. In this case, you will be treating the subsection that you choose to analyze like a stand-alone essay whose argument can be isolated and analyzed.

   Answers will vary.

4–5. Writing assignments

Classroom Exercise: focus on the world

"Geeking Out" argues that new media can help young people learn more deeply by disrupting old patterns of authority and knowledge. Ask students to reflect on their own learning experiences and to describe a time or two when they remember learning something. Have the class share some of their moments. What patterns can they detect? What are the common situations that led to learning?

Neal Conan, Kim Zetter, Andy Carvin, and Callers — *Is Creating a Fake Online Profile a Criminal Act?* pp. 699–713

1. The discussion in this transcript reminds us that stasis theory is alive and well in contemporary America. (For a discussion of stasis

theory, see Chapter 1.) In fact, U.S. legal argumentation is based on stasis theory: one must establish that something indeed happened, one must be able to define the events in terms of categories of the law, one must then be able to evaluate the events in light of the categories set up by the law, and finally one must propose a course of action—a judgement. There is general agreement—at least among the public—that "Lori Drew did something that was reprehensible" (paragraph 5), a question of fact, but there was and is no agreement about the exact nature of what she did in light of existing categories of the law. According to the transcript, why are laws relating to free speech not applicable in this case? How did this fact lead federal prosecutors in Los Angeles to charge Drew with violations of the Federal Computer Fraud and Abuse Act?

Free speech does not apply because Lori Drew was not tried for breaking laws related to what she said or wrote, so prosecutors brought a case about computer access.

What was the outcome? Why did that outcome leave so many people disappointed?

Drew was found guilty of misdemeanor charges of unauthorized access but not guilty of felony charges of intent to inflict emotional distress. Many people were unhappy because they wanted to see Drew punished more harshly; many people were also disappointed because it seems that almost anyone could be tried for not reading terms of service.

2. Andy Carvin notes that federal prosecutors chose to frame the questions at issue in the case in such a way that "Internet advocates on both the left and the right" were angered "because it raises these very complex issues of what it means to participate in the online sites and what kind of protection you have to protect you own rights" (paragraph 45). What might he have in mind? In other words, why would conservatives and/or libertarians be unhappy with this case? And liberals?

   Answers may vary. All parties might be concerned about the threat to privacy rights and the potential for government interference in computer access, which might represent a threat to free speech.

3. Perhaps the most interesting caller is Nancy (paragraphs 63–77).

Read the portion of the transcript that reports her comments. Now listen to the radio program, if you have not done so, at http://www.npr.org/templates/story/story.php?storyId=97819135. Does your response to Nancy's comments change after having heard her make them? What accounts for the difference? What might this example teach us about the potential power of spoken argument?

Answers will vary, though we're likely to learn that spoken argument can communicate more nuances of emotion and therefore carry more weight.

4. Do you regularly read the terms of service agreement for social networking sites or other sites you visit? Why or why not? Do you feel that you are taking risks if you do not?

   Answers will vary.

5–6. Writing assignments

Classroom Exercise: focus on rhetoric

As is the case with the story told by the caller named Nancy, emotional arguments are often best made through narratives. Have students collect opinion pieces from partisan newsmagazines and Web sites and look for the narratives that writers include in their pieces. Ask the students to think about what patterns develop, such as what topics in particular seem to encourage the use of narratives as evidence. You might also ask students to bring in a paper that they have written for your class or for another class and revise it to include a narrative that makes a pathetic appeal.

Charles M. Blow *A Profile of Online Profiles* pp. 715–17

1. Do the findings of the research that Blow cites surprise you? Why or why not?

   Answers will vary.

2. In what ways is a "handle" an argument? What kind of argument might it be? Why might an email address like "2Hot2Handl@ . . . com" not be an appropriate address for a student to use in academic or business contexts?

   A handle is an argument in that it establishes an ethos, just as the name of a company does; therefore, a handle could

work as a definition argument. "2Hot2Handl" would be too suggestive and personal for an academic or business context.

3. According to the research that Blow cites, how are social network sites gendered—that is, how do males and females behave differently on them?

   Men tend to use social networks more for business while women use the sites to socialize. Men also tend to lie more in their profiles.

4. A comment posted on the blog by someone who signed herself (himself?) "Mom" noted that at least some of the midteen bulge in the chart may be due to underage teens lying about their age to participate in these sites. What does this observation suggest about the challenges of interpreting data, especially quantitative data?

   Quantitative data that is self-reported data can be suspicious if people have incentives to lie (underage teens have an incentive to lie in that they can't participate unless they are a certain age); all data can be manipulated; and all data can be unintentionally misread.

5. Writing assignment

Classroom Exercise: focus on the argument

Are you surprised that social network sites are gendered? Have you noticed differences in how your friends of different genders use the sites? Drawing on the evidence of the online profiles of your friends, try to make some tentative claims about how you see the communication on social network sites as gendered. Be careful to qualify your argument and provide reasonable evidence so that you don't claim that "all men" or "all women" act in particular ways.

Wrap-up Exercises for "How Many Friends Have You Made Today?"

The following exercises encourage students to think more carefully about their own use of social network sites. The questions also offer students the opportunity to create work that reflects the changes in online communication that will have undoubtedly taken place after even the very recent publication of these articles.

1. If you have experience with social network sites, think about what that experience has been like. On the whole, do you think that the time you've spent online has benefited you? How? If not, why not? Think particularly about the counterarguments to your experience that come in the readings. If you've found social network sites to be isolating, what evidence would you cite to argue against the claims that geek culture is inherently social? If you've found social network sites to be rewarding, how would you respond to those who wrote to the *New York Times* with worries about the effects of social network sites?

2. Talk to people you know—friends, siblings, parents, teachers, and so on—who are on social network sites and in the professional world. Do they take extra care to control what goes into their online profile? Have they adopted any tactics to enhance their online ethos? Do they place special limits on who can be their friends online? Do they use Twitter or another mode of communication that doesn't get mentioned in this chapter? Come up with a set of practical guidelines—perhaps organized as a proposal argument—for presenting one's identity online that relies on what you may have learned from this chapter but that is more up-to-date and more specific than what this chapter offers.

3. Do social network sites encourage particular kinds of argument? Track the posts that some of your friends include with their online profiles. Do you see evidence that, for example, Rogerian argument is more common on social network sites than it is on, say, cable news networks? Do blogs differ from social network sites? The premise of this book is that everything is an argument, but not all arguments are alike. Spend some time researching how arguments get made online, and prepare a rhetorical analysis or evaluative argument that studies a particular site or set of sites to see how the medium shapes the messages.

What's It Like to Be Bilingual in the United States?

The readings in this chapter focus on issues relating to language and its varieties, and how we decide when, where, and with whom to speak different languages. The readings remind us that issues of language and identity are all around us, in every conversation and every text. In all of these cases, language functions as a tool for communicating information about the world and as a symbol of who we—as speakers, signers, or writers—are or wish to be. Part of the meaning of any variety of language is its value in various linguistic "markets"—on the street, in communities where it is spoken, in communities where it isn't, in the classroom, on the basketball court, during prayers. The decision to use English or another language must take into account much more than simply which language one prefers.

If we take language as a prism through which to view identity (and hence society), we appreciate how challenging it is to negotiate common ground on which to construct our arguments about language. As these texts remind us, however, if thoughtful arguments about language are to take place, we have no choice but to struggle with these challenges. These texts also remind us of the need to engage in such arguments. In this regard, they show us that language is not different from many other sources of social difference in our society.

Rochelle Sharpe *English Loses Ground* pp. 721–22

1. What argument(s) does Sharpe seem to be making? Does she have an explicit thesis? Does she believe that the changes she documents are for the better or the worse, or is it impossible to tell?

   Answers may vary, but Sharpe is certainly making an argument of fact about languages spoken in the United States. There's likely to be disagreement about whether she thinks the changes are good or bad; ask students to provide evi-

dence. They may discover that their sense of the argument depends heavily on their own beliefs and claims about language.

Is the title appropriate for this article? Why or why not?

Answers will vary, but note that the title implies that something bad is happening to the English language and its place in the world.

2. How does the information in the two final paragraphs complicate efforts to answer question 1? In what ways do these paragraphs seem to be functioning as causal arguments? From this perspective, what forces or situations are cast as causes and which as results? (For a discussion of causal arguments, see Chapter 11.)

   The last two paragraphs highlight a desire to learn English among non-English speakers and various laws that would potentially punish people who have not yet had the chance to learn English. Sharpe seems to suggest that laws designed to protect English have actually made it harder for many people to learn the language.

3. Not surprisingly, in an article from a series entitled "By the Numbers," Sharpe uses many statistics. How effectively has she used them? (For a discussion of the use of statistics, see Chapter 4.)

   Answers will vary.

4. Sharpe appears to make some interesting assumptions about language knowledge and language use. In paragraph 5, for example, she writes: "And in some pockets of the country, it's rare to hear English at all. In Hialeah, Fla., just 7.5% of its residents spoke English at home in 2000." Should we assume that those who report speaking a language other than English at home are unable to speak English at all? That they do not speak it in public at least on some occasions?

   We probably should not assume that the language people speak at home is their only language.

   For those who report speaking English and another language, why might their home be the context in which they are most likely to report using their heritage language? The context in which they are most likely to use the heritage language?

The more personal, intimate context of a home is likely to be the time when people speak their native or heritage language, and most respondents to the survey are probably answering honestly.

5. Part of the data on which Sharpe bases this article almost surely come from what was at the time a recent census report concerning the 2005–2007 American Community Survey. (Because Sharpe did not give the source of her statistics, we had to do our best to locate it.) You may view these data at http://factfinder.census.gov/servlet/STTable?_bm=y&-geo_id=01000US&-qr_name=ACS_2007_3YR_G00_S1601&-ds, the URL for "S1601. Language Spoken at Home, 2005–2007 American Community Survey Three-Year Estimates." You can find the statistic with which Sharpe begins the article under "Total" in the third row down (19.5 percent). Looking along the same row, "Speaks a language other than English," you will note that 55.7 percent of those who report speaking a language other than English at home also report speaking English "very well." Might this have been a relevant piece of data to include in Sharpe's article? Why or why not? How does this latter statistic present a more complicated picture than the overall impression given by Sharpe's article or its title? (If you are interested, the sources of data for most, if not all, of her other statistics are almost assuredly these available at http://factfinder.census.gov/servlet/ACSSAFFPeople?_submenuId=people_8&_sse=on under "Language."

   Answers will vary, but Sharpe's claim about it being rare to even hear English in Hialeah, Florida, seems almost irresponsible in light of these figures; the reality seems much more complex than the article suggests.

6. Writing assignment

Classroom Exercise: focus on the argument

Do non-English speakers in America have an obligation to learn English? Do English speakers have an obligation to teach them? Under what circumstances do you feel that the federal or state government should make English classes available to non-English-speaking immigrants? What responsibility do non-English-speaking immigrants have to learn the language on their own? In an ideal world, what do you think the official policy of your state (or the whole country) should be?

Hyon B. Shin with Rosalind Bruno *Language Use and English-Speaking Ability: 2000* pp. 724–41

1. What kind of argument—factual, definitional, evaluative, causal, or proposal—does this selection represent? What evidence would you offer?

   A factual argument. Students might cite the early description of the report as one "that presents population and housing data" and one "that describes population distributions and characteristics." They might also cite the lack of policy proposals or discussions of how to interpret or think about the data.

   Why should we expect such arguments from the U.S. Census Bureau, whose logo includes the statement "Helping You Make Informed Decisions"? (For a discussion of kinds of argument, see Chapter 1.)

   The logo suggests that the Census Bureau stops at the stasis of fact so that lawmakers and others have facts with which to discuss appropriate policy, which will be based on definitions, evaluations, causal arguments, and proposals.

2. This report was produced by the U.S. Census Bureau. How does that fact itself represent an ethical appeal? For example, how might it influence your evaluation of the credibility of this report as a source you might use for constructing an academic argument? (For a discussion of ethical appeals, see Chapter 3. For a discussion of evaluating sources, see Chapter 19.)

   The U.S. Census Bureau, having had its purpose outlined in the Constitution, has long had a reputation as a responsible, nonpartisan organization, though political groups have certainly challenged that nonpartisan stance. The U.S. Census Bureau is likely to seem very credible for an academic argument because of its long history and its nonpartisan reputation.

3. Examine Figure 5 carefully. What is the value of presenting the data in two ways—by county (the larger map) and by state (the smaller map inset in the upper right-hand corner)? (The island in the lower right-hand corner is Puerto Rico.) What do these two presentations of the same data remind us about the nature of vi-

sual arguments? (For a discussion of visual arguments, see Chapter 14.)

The examples of Illinois and New York perhaps best illustrate how the state map can suggest that dense concentrations of those not speaking English at home—in these cases found primarily in Chicago and New York City—affect the percentages of the whole state. This comparison reminds us that visual arguments must be considered as carefully as any other; they can distort information in the same ways that other arguments can.

4. Note 5 explains the use of the term "non-English-speaker," while the shaded box on p. 736 provides definitions for the terms "linguistically isolated household" and "linguistically isolated person." What kinds of definitions are these? (For a discussion of kinds of definitions, see Chapter 9.)

   Operational definitions.

   Demographers need category labels, but these labels have received criticism from social scientists who study issues of language in society. What might their complaints be? In other words, in what ways might these labels be seen as inaccurate, unfair, and perhaps even prejudicial?

   Answers will vary, but "non-English-speaker" makes it sound as though the speaker does not know English even though it's meant only to describe an individual's linguistic behavior at home. "Linguistically isolated person" may suggest a way of life that does not accord with the speaker's reality; a Spanish speaker in Hialeah, Florida (near Miami), for example, is not likely to feel linguistically isolated. Many of the areas that are home to "linguistically isolated persons" are in fact densely populated with people who share a common language other than English.

   Why is this question of special relevance in a report of this kind?

   These issues are relevant because the census claims not to be making value judgments, but these terms imply that not speaking English might be a deficiency.

5. The next-to-last section of the report is entitled "Accuracy of the Estimates." Why is this information useful or even necessary to

readers? How do these qualifications (that is, instances of qualifying the claims made) strengthen the argument? The credibility of the report? The ethos of the authors? (For a discussion of qualifying claims, see Chapter 7.)

Answers may vary, but this information certainly helps people understand the process that the researchers used and its limitations. The writers likely seem more authoritative because they're aware of the precise possibility of error and they have acknowledged potential rebuttals.

6. Writing assignment

Classroom Exercise: focus on rhetoric

Brainstorm alternative terms for "linguistically isolated household" and "linguistically isolated person" that the Census Bureau could use. After you've created a list, go over it with other members of your class to discuss the possible implications of your suggested terms. How many neutral terms can you come up with? Does this exercise make you more or less sympathetic with the task faced by the Census Bureau?

Sandra Cisneros *From "Bien Pretty"* pp. 743–44

1. For Cisneros—and one can likely claim it for all bilinguals—in some sense the languages she knows aren't equal. Rather, each language is associated with different worlds of experience. What does Spanish connote for the narrator in Cisneros's text? What does English connote? Where would such connotations come from?

   Spanish connotes memories from home and family life because it is the language she grew up with, the language spoken inside her home. English has harsh, stiff connotations, "starched r's and g's" (paragraph 5), likely because she grew up with it being used for official business with those outside of her family and community.

2. One resource bilingual writers have is code switching—switching between the languages they know. In this excerpt, we see the simple noun phrase "la Alhambra" (paragraph 4) from Spanish, which we can correctly understand even if we know no Spanish. We also see the phrase "*Ya, ya, ya*" (paragraph 9), which is followed immediately by the English equivalent, "There, there, there." Yet we

also find the phrases "*mi vida, mi preciosa, mi chiquitita*" (paragraph 4), which we may not be able to figure out the meanings of. (In fact, the phrases translate literally as "my life, my precious [one], my dearest little [one]"—things native speakers of English wouldn't normally say to one another, even when being intimate. Such phrases are perfectly normal among speakers of Spanish.) Why might writers purposely create texts that include parts readers may not be able to understand? Why would such a strategy be especially effective when talking about intimacies like making love?

Writers might use code switching to mirror their normal speech patterns among bilingual friends and family. In addition, they might want to leave some elements of their story out of their reader's comprehension. For Cisneros, lovemaking remains a private act because her English-speaking readers cannot understand Flavio's sweet nothings.

3. Writing assignment

Classroom Exercise: focus on style

Using Chapter 13 (Style in Arguments) as a guide, analyze Cisneros's use of figurative language. How does she use literary tropes such as metaphors, similes, and analogies to make her writing more compelling? How does she use syntactic schemes for the same purpose? What sentences, phrases, paragraphs, or ideas do you find most striking? Why? How does her writing style affect your reading, understanding, analysis, and evaluation of her argument?

Marjorie Agosín *Always Living in Spanish* pp. 745–47

Marjorie Agosín *English* pp. 748–50

1. Why does Agosín write only in Spanish? How do her reasons for using Spanish compare with those of Cisneros? How does she regard using Spanish as relating to her ancestry as a Jew?

   She writes only in Spanish to keep the memories of her childhood alive. She and Cisneros both see Spanish as connected with their families, with their community, and with their homes. Growing up in a Jewish family that was forced to flee, Agosín sees language as a key to memory, often the

only way to remember what you were forced to leave behind.

2. What sort of experiences did Agosín have while trying to learn English? How typical do you think her experiences were? In other words, how do Americans who are native speakers of English treat nonnative speakers of English? How did Spanish represent a source of strength and consolation to Agosín during the period when she was learning English?

   She was ridiculed and insulted, and she constantly felt the need to explain to English speakers why her English was so poor. She was treated as an outsider and given less respect than a native speaker of English was given. Spanish was a strength and consolation because it connected her with her identity, the world she left behind, the security of her family, and the space in which she belonged.

3. What does Spanish represent for Agosín? Why would it represent these things for her?

   Answers will vary but might include the notion that Spanish represents many of her memories from Chile—plants and flowers, family, friendship, warmth. It represents these things because it's connected to her memories of childhood and to her nostalgia for the country and family she left behind.

4. Writing assignment

Classroom Exercise: focus on the argument

How is Agosín's poem similar to and different from her essay? How does one text help you understand the other? What argument does each make? Do you think one is more effective than the other? Why? Why would the editors of this textbook choose to include both the essay and the poem?

Firoozeh Dumas *The "F Word"* pp. 751–55

1. How might you summarize Firoozeh Dumas's argument? What's its subject—the importance of names, the ways in which Americans have traditionally responded to unfamiliar names, the immigrant experience, all of these?

Dumas's argument is that a name is an integral part of human identity. The subject of the article is how Americans respond to names and what they assume from names. This look at names is interesting because it's from an immigrant's point of view.

2. Carefully reread paragraph 12 of the essay, in which Dumas explains how having an "American" name and speaking English without a foreign accent was like having "X-ray glasses." Is Dumas's portrayal of Americans in this passage and elsewhere in the essay flattering? Humorous? Honest? In this passage, Dumas notes that "people assumed I was American." What definition of "American" must she (and those she writes about) be assuming?

   Dumas talks about certain people's responses to her when assuming she was American. These people and those that avoid pronouncing foreign names (Americans) are not portrayed in a positive light. "American" is conversely broadened to apparently mean someone born in the United States who speaks English without an accent.

   Is such a definition valid, given evidence she presents elsewhere in the essay and the fact that the United States is often called a nation of immigrants? At what point does an immigrant become an American?

   Answers will vary.

3. How would you describe Dumas's use of humor? Find three examples that you especially like, and explain how the humor helps the author achieve her goals. In what ways does Dumas's argument represent satire, with the simultaneous goals of ridiculing and remedying a problematic situation? (For a discussion of the uses of humor in argumentation, see Chapter 2.)

   Answers will vary.

4. How does Dumas use the repeated metaphor of the spice cabinet to help structure her argument? Why is this metaphor an appropriate one, given her topic? How does the metaphor permit her to critique the mother who called her "F Word" (paragraph 17)?

   The metaphor of spice can be used to talk about the sounds of language, cultural experiences, comforts, and the willingness to try new things. This usage is particularly appro-

priate for her topic and allows her to accuse the mother from her children's school of refusing to add to her spice cabinet.

5. Writing assignment

Classroom Exercise: focus on the world

Have students ever chosen a new name in a language class? How did they feel about that? Have they ever traveled to a foreign country and changed the pronunciation of their name or chosen a whole new name to make other people feel more comfortable? To fit in better? Have they chosen to keep their own name even when the pronunciation is very different from the host language? Was it frustrating to hear their name presented so differently? What is it about our names—which are just words, after all—that hold so much personal identity and meaning?

Lan Cao *The Gift of Language* pp. 756–62

1. What's your initial response to this excerpt from Cao's novel? Given the mother's cultural expectations, which she has brought from Vietnam, is it logical for her to respond as she does?

   Answers will vary.

   In what senses is Cao forced to parent her mother?

   She must teach her mother how to behave appropriately in the United States.

2. How does Cao construct the argument she makes here? What sorts of evidence does she rely on? How does she use language effectively to convey her ideas? (Chapters 7, 16, and 13, respectively, will help you answer these questions.)

   Cao uses specific incidents, such as their experience buying pork at the supermarket, to describe the process of immigrating and the effect it had on her relationship with her mother. She uses vivid descriptions of the American and Vietnamese markets to note their extreme differences.

3. The tale that Cao tells has been told many times in the writings of immigrants, especially those who arrive in the United States as children with parents who speak little or no English. What are the con-

sequences for family life? How does language become a source of power for the child? How does this power disrupt the traditional patterns of family life?

Family dynamics shift. Children must grow up fast and be able to explain the ways of this new country to their parents, and parents must accept the authority of their children.

4. Writing assignment

Classroom Exercise: focus on rhetoric

Although this is an excerpt from a novel, Cao makes a clear argument here. Conduct a Toulmin analysis of Cao's argument. What is her claim? What are her reasons? What are her grounds to support her claim? What are her underlying warrants, and what backing does she provide for them? Does she provide any qualifiers and rebuttals? Do you think her argument is effective or ineffective? Why? How does the fact that this is an excerpt from a novel affect your analysis of the argument?

Amy Tan *Mother Tongue* pp. 763–68

1. How have Tan's attitudes toward her mother's English changed over the years? Why?

   She has learned that her mother's English is not "broken," and she is no longer ashamed. She understands that having language-learner's grammar or accent does not diminish the quality of her mother's thoughts.

   In what ways does Tan describe a situation that probably is faced by most children of immigrants?

   Many children of immigrants probably feel caught between too cultures, and their parents' difficulty with English may force them into situations and roles that they don't feel prepared for.

   In what ways is this situation like or unlike the embarrassment that children generally feel about their parents at some point in their growing up?

   Answers will vary.

2. Why is Tan suspicious of language ability tests? What are her complaints?

   She is suspicious of these tests because they can't measure richness of language use or of language perception. She is uncomfortable because the test questions have only one correct answer, as though they are math questions.

   What sorts of evidence does she offer?

   She uses an extended example of the limitations of analogy questions. These questions aim at only one specific relationship between two words even though there may be others. The person who perceives that richness is penalized.

   Do you agree or disagree with her argument? Why?

   Answers will vary.

3. Tan's text was written to be read aloud by the author herself. In what ways might this fact be important? (For a discussion of the features of arguments to be heard, see Chapter 15.)

   Spoken texts require more and different signposts to help listeners keep track of the structure. They usually use simple sentences. Informal language is usually more acceptable in spoken texts.

   What would it be like, for example, to have heard Tan deliver this text? How would such an experience have been different from reading it on the page? Had Tan written the piece to be read silently by strangers—as her novels are, for example—how might she have altered it? Why?

   Answers will vary.

4. Writing assignment

Classroom Exercise: focus on rhetoric

Amy Tan and Lan Cao both write about their mothers and their mothers' language. Compare and contrast the ways in which these writers use their mothers' language and experiences with languages as part of their argument.

Making a Visual Argument: Public Service Announcements in Spanish

National Institute of Mental Health *En la comunidad latina tenemos una cultura de silencio* p. 770

Agency for Healthcare Research and Quality *Non eres un superheroe* p. 771

1. Both of these posters use Spanish, either predominately or completely. Why? How do language choice and targeted audience interact in these advertisements?

   This advertisement seems to target Hispanic men because mental health is a shameful topic in that community, especially among men. The choice of Spanish makes it clear even to bilingual men that the message is for them.

   Many Hispanic Americans are highly bilingual, although some of them prefer English, some prefer Spanish, and others have no preference. On the other hand, some Hispanic Americans speak little or no English, and still others speak little or no Spanish. How does this situation complicate efforts to create advertisements that target the Hispanic community?

   The multitude of language preferences makes it hard to figure out how to appeal to the largest number of potential audience members.

2. Evaluate each of these ads as an argument. In "*En la comunidad latina tenemos una cultura de silencio*," what role does the personal testimony of Rodolfo Palma-Lulión play in the advertisement? Does it matter that he is a university student? Why or why not?

   The testimony of Palma-Lulión allows the male audience to relate to him as another man. As a university student he represents someone who is educated and successful and yet struggles with depression.

   Why might the designers have included the phrase "Real Men. Real Depression" in English?

   "Real Men. Real Depression" may be the official motto of the campaign to reach men in all languages. The subtle code switching might also reach bilingual men.

In "*No eres un superheroe*," what are the links between the text and the visual images?

The figure in the image has the pose of a superhero as he pulls his clothes back; a superhero, however, would reveal his costume under his clothes. In this image, the man reveals a normal human chest that can benefit from the medical attention of a doctor.

3. Some might criticize these U.S. government agencies or the Ad Council for producing advertisements or running programs in any language other than English. What arguments might they use for such criticisms? What costs, direct or indirect, might there be if U.S. government agencies do not produce advertisements or design programs in languages other than English? (If you're having trouble with this question, you might visit the Web site for the Ad Council ad for the AHRQ, which explains the need for an ad campaign focused on this topic for this audience.)

   The agencies behind these ads use different languages to reach different audiences that need their help. Not addressing audiences that do not speak English would leave a large section of the population without services and could mean that more emergency services would be required in the future.

4. Writing assignment

Classroom Exercise: focus on the world

Some argue that American advertisements and public-service announcements should be presented in English and that presenting them in other languages enables people to avoid learning English. Why would public-service agencies create a Spanish-language campaign? Why might a business make advertisements in other languages? Does this sound like a good business practice? How would you react to people from Miami or Los Angeles who felt that Spanish advertising was invading their cityscape?

Amy Martinez Starke *Hmong Elder Didn't Forget the Old Ways* pp. 773–76

1. How is Sao Yee Cha's bilingualism like and unlike that of others whose experiences have been described in this chapter?

Most of the others in this chapter (Cisneros, Tan, Cao, Dumas, and Agosín) are all fluent in at least two languages and highly literate in English; all learned English at a younger age and are fluent in English, even, with the exception of Agosín, choosing it as the primary language in which they write. Like Sao Yee Cha, though, all have felt separated from the mainstream English-speaking culture that has surrounded them.

2. What sort of occasion gives rise to an obituary—forensic, deliberative, or epideictic? (The answer may be more complex than it seems. For a discussion of occasions for argument, see Chapter 1.)

   Obituaries are most commonly epideictic or ceremonial arguments, but they could easily be forensic arguments that attempt to make sense of what happened in the past. They're unlikely to be deliberative, though it's not impossible, as a speaker might want to use the example of someone else's life as a spur to pursue a future action.

3. In what ways do the illustrations that accompany this selection form part of the argument? What do they contribute to the force of the argument? (For a discussion of visual arguments, see Chapter 14.)

   Answers will vary, but may include how the images highlight, especially in the clothing and the surroundings, the vast differences between the two cultures Sao Yee Cha lived in.

4–5. Writing assignments

Classroom Exercise: focus on the world

Obituaries are commonly epideictic arguments; that is, they seek to praise or blame someone for their character or accomplishments or lack thereof. Try your hand at crafting an epideictic text—praise or blame a person, place, or thing. To add some extra interest to your piece, consider working against the conventional wisdom about your subject—praise someone or something we might ordinarily think of as deserving blame, or blame someone or something we normally praise.

Wrap-up Exercises for "What's It Like to Be Bilingual in the United States?"

These assignments are suggested as wrap-up exercises in which students can integrate any or all of the readings of the chapter. Either would be suitable for an in-class essay assignment.

1. Write an essay in which you take to task the writer whose argument you find least convincing among those you read in this chapter. In other words, critique that writer's argument, demonstrating why your perspective on the topic is better supported. One of your tasks as a writer will be to summarize the argument you're critiquing so that readers unfamiliar with the original text will understand both the original writer's position and yours.

2. Write an argument about language(s) and identities in which you incorporate your own experiences as a user of the language varieties you know (or those you do not know). How, for example, do you imagine your life might be different if you knew certain languages or certain varieties of English, or how would it be different if you did not know the language(s) or varieties that you do? How would the command of these linguistic varieties shape your identity as an individual or as a member of the groups to which you belong?

   Another way of imagining this assignment, if you are monolingual, is to think about what your life would have been like if you'd grown up in a community where a language other than English was used (perhaps exclusively, perhaps in addition to English). What challenges might you have faced thus far with respect to mastering the language(s) of your home community? Those used outside the home community? How might dealing with these challenges have influenced the way you perceive yourself both inside and outside the community? Similarly, if you grew up bilingually, imagine what your life would be like if you were monolingual. How would you be different?

Why Worry about Food and Water?

Everyone eats, and the readings in this chapter reflect a belief that this activity of consuming that takes up so much of our time and energy deserves more careful consideration. The readings encourage students to think more seriously not only about the food that they choose to eat but also about how food choices fit into larger patterns of culture and consumption. Though food has become a popular topic of debate, and though Americans seem to be thinking more about their food and its origins than they did before, students probably still come to our classes without thinking of food as a major issue for debate. This chapter therefore gives them rich opportunities to explore an area they know quite a lot about but which may not have been framed for them in the ways that these readings do. Some of the questions that the chapter encourages us to ask include:

- Beyond satisfying our hunger and thirst, what should we think about when we think about food and water?
- What responsibilities to our communities and to the environment do our food choices reflect?
- How do we even understand what it means to eat and drink responsibly in a world where much of what we consume comes through corporate intermediaries?

Mark Bittman *Why Take Food Seriously?* pp. 779–82

1. In what ways is Americans' relationship with food changing, according to Bittman?

   Bittman argues that Americans are taking food more seriously, by which he means that they have become more interested in where their food comes from and how it is prepared.

   What evidence does he provide?

His evidence is the rise of food television and celebrity chefs, the nature of American conversations about food, the interest shown in food by young people, and the increased range of international cooking (and immigrant populations who have helped fuel that trend).

For Bittman, what is the good news about our relationship with food?

Bittman values Americans' heightened awareness of what they're eating.

The bad news?

Overconsumption of meat is endangering the environment, the seas are overfished, factory farming of animals has harmed good eating practices, and obesity and foodborne illnesses remain threatening.

2. You are one of the real readers of Bittman's argument. Who were his intended readers—that is, what kind of readers did Bittman assume would read this text? How do you know?

   The article appeared in the *New York Times Sunday Magazine*, a relatively sophisticated publication. His intended audience probably thinks about food a great deal and has quite a bit of experience with fine food.

   Who were the invoked readers—that is, those who are represented in the text?

   Bittman invokes all Americans as readers since all of them eat. Part of the evidence that he's speaking to all Americans is his use of plural first-person pronouns (e.g., "We are taking food seriously again").

   What kinds of experience and knowledge do they have? What are their values? Provide evidence from the text for your claims. (For a discussion of categories of audiences, see Chapter 1.)

   Most of his intended and invoked readers have a great deal of knowledge of food and cooking; some textual evidence would include his assumption that readers will be familiar with food figures such as Julia Child and Paul Bocuse.

3. How have changing gender roles influenced Americans' relation-

ship with food, according to Bittman? Do you agree? Why or why not?

4. Examine the chart labeled "Fast-Food Nations." Based on this sample of nine nations, where does the Unied States fall in "meals eaten out per person" (meaning meals prepared by restaurants)?

   The U.S. has the second highest total of meals eaten out of the home.

   What relationship, if any, is there between this chart and Bittman's argument?

   Bittman sees preparing meals at home as part of a serious and responsible food culture; he would probably like to see more meals prepared and eaten at home.

   How representative is your behavior of the behavior of most Americans? In other words, is it likely you ate more or fewer than 120 meals or so out (or from restaurants) in 2005? How does your behavior compare with that of your classmates? What accounts for the differences? The similarities?

   Answers will vary.

5. Writing assignment

Classroom Exercise: focus on the world

Ask students to view one or more cooking shows on television or to think more carefully about cooking shows that they have seen. In what ways does celebrity affect the show and the food that the hosts prepare? How does the host talk about food? What values about food does the show seem to hold and promote? In class, have students talk about how different hosts approach food so that the class can understand what it means to have different approaches to and values about food.

Wynne Wright and Gerad Middendorf *Introduction: Fighting over Food—Change in the Agrifood System* pp. 784–92

1. According to Wright and Middendorf, what social forces have led to our fights over food—that is, to the changing relationships between Americans and food?

The authors focus on people who resist the corporatization and industrialization of food brought about by agribusiness.

Which of these forces were you aware of before reading this selection? What might account for your awareness or lack of awareness of them?

Answers will vary.

2. Where are the areas of overlap and difference between Wright and Middendorf's analysis of our changing relationship with food and Mark Bittman's analysis in the previous selection, "Why Take Food Seriously? Because Your Life Depends on It"?

   The articles overlap in their concern with recent changes in the attention paid to eating and where food comes from. Bittman focuses more on how chefs and cookbook authors have helped shape changes in our eating; Wright and Middendorf emphasize the problems created by agribusiness.

   What might be the sources of those differences?

   One possibility is that Bittman, himself something of a food celebrity (he has a weekly column in the *New York Times*, several successful cookbooks, and his own cooking show on PBS), is more concerned with how celebrity chefs and cookbook authors have shaped food trends.

3. Legal debates often involve arguments about definitions. In what ways do the raw milk, cow-share cooperatives (paragraph 1) demonstrate how individuals and groups use definitional arguments to obey the letter of the law but avoid satisfying the intent of the law?

   The definition most at stake is what it means to "own" a cow.

4. As the headnote explains, this selection is from the introductory chapter of a book of articles that were written by academic researchers about issues related to food. What cues in the text tell the reader that this selection is part of an introduction? In other words, what do readers expect the introduction of a book to do, and how does this particular selection fulfill those expectations?

   The authors provide an overview of what issues and topics the rest of the text will address, provide a history of what is

already known about the topic, and establish what is at stake in the argument that the book presents.

5. Writing assignment

Classroom Exercise: focus on the argument

As a class, research the issue of how agribusiness affects food. A good starting point is Culinate.com's collection of ten Web sites about sustainable food, available at http:// www.culinate.com/articles/features/sustainable_food_resouces_online, but you should also encourage students to seek out defenses of industrial agriculture, such as farmer Blake Hurst's article from the magazine of the American Enterprise Institute, available at http://www.american.com/ archive/2009/july/the-omnivore2019s-delusion-against-the-agri-intellectuals. Use the information that the students gather to stage a debate in class.

Solomon H. Katz *The World Food Crisis: An Overview of the Causes and Consequences* pp. 794–98

1. It is fairly easy to analyze this essay as a proposal argument. What is Katz proposing?

   Katz proposes that anthropologists should study how food and culture interact to help solve problems associated with food production and supply.

   Why is it appropriate for him to make such a proposal to anthropologists? If you're not sure what anthropologists study, research that topic before answering the question. (For a discussion of proposal arguments, see Chapter 12.)

   He writes to anthropologists because they have the skill set and disciplinary experience to make sense of how food and culture interact.

2. Like all good proposal arguments, this one makes a strong case that a problem needs to be solved. In defining that problem, Katz lays out several complex causal arguments, which are often a feature of proposal arguments. What are those arguments, and how might they be characterized?

   Katz makes far-reaching causal arguments for problems with the world food supply, including: increases in popula-

tion; improvements in agricultural productivity that led people to move to cities; the rise of global food distribution; major food crop production becoming dependent on technological advances (especially hybrid seeds and fertilizer); and global warming's changing of weather patterns. All of these factors have affected agricultural productivity or the global food supply.

More recent causes for problems with the world food supply that Katz describes include: a global wheat shortage caused by an Australian drought; a rise in U.S. corn prices because of the incentives to create ethanol from corn; a decline in soybean production caused by the increased planting of corn for ethanol; a rise in food costs for livestock farmers and a subsequent rise in prices of animal products; the rise in the price of palm oil because of EU encouragement of biofuels; and food hoarding and speculation. All of these factors have helped raise the price of food.

Katz's causal arguments are complex and interrelated, based at least partly on definitions, and yield probable rather than absolute conclusions.

After you have a list, categorize the causes and effects by reprsenting them visually as illustrated in "Understanding Causal Arguments" in Chapter 11.

Answers will vary.

3. Why might Katz have arranged his argument in the order he did?

   Katz seeks to establish the problem as a global problem, with many interrelated causes tied to cultural differences and economic and environmental influences.

   Would the selection have been as successful if, for example, he had begun by discussing the recent causes of the world food crisis rather than beginning with what he terms "The Macro Picture"? Why or why not?

   Answers may vary, though we believe that he needs to establish the significance of the problem in "The Macro Picture" before he identifies causes.

4. Accompanying Katz's essay is a sidebar titled "Food Crisis Information and Resources." Why might the editors of *Anthropology*

News have included this information in their series on the world food crisis?

The sidebar makes a logical argument for how a reader can get more information, and it enhances the ethos of the publication by proclaiming their ongoing concern for the issue.

How would you characterize it as an argument? (Is it, for example, definitional or evaluative?)

The sidebar might be characterized as a proposal argument that argues that anthropologists should attend the meeting and should keep up-to-date on the world food crisis.

Why do you think that the editors recommended electronic rather than print resources?

Electronic sources are constantly updated and so can report on the most recent trends and news concerning food; the editors hope to underscore that the issue is ongoing and constantly changing.

5. Writing assignment

Classroom Exercise: focus on the world

Ask students to think of their own food traditions and what role food plays in their cultural traditions. How do these traditions interact with the culture around them? Do their traditions help them feel a sense of belonging? Do they make them feel isolated from others? Can they articulate any ways that their own traditions affect the world food supply or other food issues outside their own immediate sphere?

Kathy Freston *Vegetarian Is the New Prius* pp. 800–803

1. For Freston, why is vegetarianism the new Prius? How does she compare a diet with an automobile and use the comparison to her advantage?

   Freston argues that vegetarianism is a popular trend that both benefits the earth and displays one's commitment to things that benefit the earth.

2. In what ways is Freston's argument a proposal argument? An evaluative argument?

Freston is proposing that people become vegetarians as a way of helping the environment, and she evaluates different ways of making a difference in the environment—in this case, she determines that eating a vegetarian diet is more helpful than driving a hybrid.

Why do we expect all proposal arguments to contain evaluative elements even if they aren't full evaluative arguments? (For a discussion of evaluative arguments, see Chapter 10. For a discussion of proposal arguments, see Chapter 12.)

A proposal argument contains evaluative claims because it is crucial to show that your proposal is better and more important than others—a proposal argument needs to evaluate the desirability of other potential solutions to arrive at an argument about which is the best one.

3. In American journalism and in Internet postings like Freston's, writers often do not provide references or sources for their statistics. Using the Internet, try to find evidence that either supports or calls into question three of the statistics that Freston uses.

   Answers will vary.

4. As is also common in such Internet postings, Freston uses informal language, including conversational sentence structures and wording that would not be appropriate in academic writing. Working with a classmate, find at least three examples of her informal language and revise them to convey the same information in ways that are appropriate for academic writing generally. If you're having trouble with this question, compare the language in this selection to that in the previous one, Solomon H. Katz's "The World Food Crisis: An Overview of the Causes and Consequences," which is written in a formal, academic style. (For a discussion of academic argument, see Chapter 6. For a discussion of style in argument, see Chapter 13, especially the first few sections of the chapter.)

   Answers will vary.

5. Study the cartoon on p. 804, which gives three reasons a person might be or become vegetarian. In light of this cartoon, how would you characterize Freston's reasons for becoming and remaining vegetarian? What arguments could someone make in support of becoming vegetarian for each of the three reasons given in the cartoon? How does the fact that carnivores—people who eat meat—

sometimes suspect that at least some vegetarians avoid eating meat "just to annoy people" create an extra burden for those arguing in support of vegetarianism?

Answers will vary.

6. Writing assignment

Classroom Exercise: focus on the argument

Do you find Freston's argument persuasive? If so, why? If not, why not? What do you think are the best arguments for vegetarianism? What are the best arguments against a vegetarian diet? Are there any provegetarian arguments that you think your peers would find persuasive?

Making a Visual Argument

Claire Ironside *Apples to Oranges* pp. 805–15

1. What is Ironside's explicit argument?

   Her explicit argument is that food brought in from a distance requires more fossil-fuel consumption than food grown more locally.

   What kind of argument is it?

   An argument of fact that is meant to inform.

   Might she be making an implicit argument? What would that argument be? And what kind of argument is it (for example, of fact or definition)?

   She might be making an implicit proposal argument that we should choose local food.

2. Analyze each pair of pages in Ironside's argument. What does each juxtaposition contribute to her argument?

   The first two pages introduce us to the idea of comparing apples and oranges (an ironic choice given that the phrase "apples and oranges" is usually meant to describe things that shouldn't be compared). The second two pages offer us a graphic representation and a verbal explanation of how

many fossil-fuel calories we expend on average for each food calorie we consume, thus giving us a context where we might hope to be able to reduce the input of fossil fuels. The third pair of images dramatically illustrates the difference in distance traveled for a local apple versus a California orange, making it somewhat more concrete than if we had only heard the difference stated in numbers. The fourth image allows us to see the difference in how the fossil-fuel inputs contribute to the delivery of the food and where the energy goes (reactions will vary, but we wonder if this image might not confuse some readers, since the previous image makes a much more clear-cut argument). The final image illustrates the overall difference in fossil-fuel consumption for each piece of fruit compared to average.

How would you characterize the purpose of the comparison related to fossil-fuel inputs?

This graphic is an argument to inform that teaches us that all food that we buy (and almost all food that we grow) requires some investment of fossil fuels, but it also tells us the differences in how those fossil-fuel inputs are allocated.

What value might there be in the details given?

Answers may vary, but we tend to think that this juxtaposition reminds us that almost all food requires fossil-fuel inputs, but that we might want those inputs to be more for things like cooking and preparation than for trucking across long distances.

What sorts of conclusions might we draw from this juxtaposition?

Answers may vary, but we lean toward a conclusion that local food generally contributes to a cleaner environment and a more sensible allocation of fossil-fuel energy.

3. Evaluate the visual aspects of Ironside's argument, including her choice of colors.

   Answers will vary.

4. Writing assignment

5. Visual argument or writing assignment

Classroom Exercise: focus on the argument

As Question 1 suggests, Ironside is likely making an implicit argument that we should eat more local food. You might ask students to detail what they ate at their last meal and try to figure out where their food came from—are they eating locally? Do they even know how to find out? You might also ask them to think about what it would mean to eat locally all the time. Would they be willing to eat produce only in season? Are there foods that must be imported that they would never give up? Are there good arguments for not worrying about eating locally?

Wikipedia *Local Food* pp. 817–29

1. In what ways is an encyclopedia entry an argument? What kind of argument is it? What evidence can you provide for your claims?

   Encyclopedia articles are generally arguments to inform an audience. In this case, the entry is largely a definition argument, laying out the criteria for which food may be considered "local food."

2. How does this Wikipedia entry contribute to your understanding of issues relating to food in the United States and the world? In what ways does it complement the previous readings in this chapter by providing new ways for thinking about the issues discussed? In what ways does it provide information that is not discussed in earlier readings? What might account for these situations?

   Answers will vary, but students might note that the article complicates the definition of "local," a word that normally would not seem to be that controversial. One important point of difference from earlier articles is that this is an argument to inform and less of an attempt to persuade or convince.

3. Labels matter. In fact, we contend that names are often arguments. What are the differences in referring to the trends described in this selection as "local food," "regional food," "food patriotism," and "the local food movement"? To answer this question, you'll need to determine the denotations and connotations of each name. Which sorts of groups might favor or disfavor each name? Why?

   Answers will vary, but "local food" is probably more limited in terms of the range of physical space involved than "re-

gional food" is. "Food patriotism" implies a connection to food that is perhaps less about a physical point of origin than it is about a political or perhaps cultural definition of a space. The "local food movement" highlights the political activism of a belief in local foods more than an interest in, for example, nutrition or freshness or flavor.

4. Compare this January 17, 2009, version of Wikipedia's "Local food" entry with the version that is posted when you read the selection. What changes have been made to the selection? (If you click on the tabs labeled "Discussion," "Edit This Page," and "History" at the top of the entry, they will provide you with information about earlier versions of the page and the discussions that led to its current version.) What does studying the discussion and history of the article teach you about evaluating it? About how knowledge is constructed in Wikipedia?

   Answers will vary, but a discussion about how knowledge is constructed in Wikipedia probably should note how dependent this site is on the idea of argument. Comparing entries from different dates reveals quickly how contested even much factual information can be. Wikipedia helps establish the point that everything is an argument because knowledge is constructed by different people contributing entries that reflect their claims and ideas—the knowledge is never fixed but always under construction.

5–6. Writing assignments

Classroom Exercise: focus on rhetoric

You can teach students a great deal about how knowledge is constructed in Wikipedia by having them contribute to articles. First, give them some time in class to brainstorm things that they know a lot about, whatever that subject may be. Next, have them read Wikipedia articles on the subjects of their expertise to look for holes—where could they add useful information or an external link that would provide background? Once they've discovered places where they can add information, have them edit articles. Students who do not have them will need to create wiki accounts and send you their usernames so that you can track their edits. Not only will students who contribute to a Wikipedia article have a deeper understanding of how knowledge is constructed there, but they are also likely to be more sensitive to the importance of evaluating sources carefully.

Mark Coleman Review of *Bottlemania: How Water Went on Sale and Why We Bought It* pp. 831–33

1. How would you characterize Mark Coleman's evaluation of Elizabeth Royte's book? Do you think that he likes the book? How well? Why? What evidence can you cite for your characterization of his evaluation?

   Overall, Coleman seems to like the book. He praises it as "tautly paced" and admires her "mordant wit" and "intellectual curiosity." Students should be able to find ample evidence of his approval of the book.

2. A review of a book (or movie or DVD or concert) is, by definition, an evaluative argument. What criteria does Coleman use in evaluating Royte's book? Do these criteria seem appropriate and sufficient to the task? Why or why not? (For a discussion of evaluative arguments, see Chapter 10.)

   Answers will vary, but some possibilities for criteria include intellectual complexity; writing that is well paced; entertainment value; pragmatism in approach to issues surrounding bottled water.

3. Coleman contends that as a writer, "Royte doesn't traffic in platitudes, moral certainties or oversimplification; she's unafraid of ambiguity" (paragraph 2). What evidence do you find for these claims in his review? Should you find any?

   Answers will vary. One possibility: Coleman notes that Royte mentions the appeal that bottled water holds even though for the most part she finds it objectionable.

4. Examine Coleman's use of quotations from Royte's book. What functions do they serve in Coleman's own argument? (In answering this question, you may wish to make a list of all the quotations to examine their functions carefully.)

   Answers will vary. Some possibilities include that they illustrate points that he makes about the quality of her writing (such as the idea that she knows how to get out of the way) while other quotations help persuade the audience that issues surrounding bottled water are important enough to be taken seriously.

5. Writing assignment

Classroom Exercise: focus on rhetoric

Many book reviews and some movie reviews do not seem to be straightforward evaluations; they don't end with recommendations to read or not to read or to view or not to view. Instead, these reviews provide an overview of the argument of the book under discussion and often contribute their own knowledge on the topic. Ask your students to try their hand at such a review. They can review a book or film (or other media production) and write an evaluation that works to understand meaning and significance as well as judge the quality of the product under review.

Elizabeth Royte Excerpt from *Bottlemania: How Water Went on Sale and Why We Bought It* pp. 834–41

1. Briefly summarize Royte's response to the question with which she begins this excerpt.

   Royte suggests that, unless we have strong reasons for concern about our water or our reactions to potential pathogens, we should probably drink our tap water; ideally, though, we should install point-of-use filters.

   How well does she support her conclusions?

   Answers will vary.

2. Summarize the arguments that are made by the *New York Times* graphic, and describe several contexts in which it could conceivably be used.

   The graphic argues that Americans consume huge quantities of bottled water, suggesting also that they are drinking less tap water. The graphic about rates of consumption could be used in marketing or in public health contexts or if a store were trying to decide what products to stock. The bottled water consumption graph might contribute to discussions about plastic recycling or solid waste handling or in marketing decisions for beverage companies.

   Evaluate the graphic's effectiveness as a visual argument. (You may wish to locate the *Times* article with which this graphic originally appeared and use that information as part of your evaluation. For a discussion of evaluative arguments, see Chapter 10. For a discussion of visual arguments, see Chapter 14.)

Answers will vary.

3. In paragraph 2 of the previous selection, Mark Coleman's review of Royte's book, Coleman claims that "Royte doesn't traffic in platitudes, moral certainties or oversimplification; she's unafraid of ambiguity." What evidence for his evaluation do you see in this excerpt from Royte's book?

   Answers will vary, but we suggest one sentence as a good piece of evidence: "Certainly, nearly everything humans do has an environmental impact—biking to work, recycling newspapers, and drinking tap water included." That sentence provides a good example of her tolerance of ambiguity since all of these activities are generally thought of as environmentally responsible.

4. One of the ways that readers know that Royte is writing for a popular audience rather than an academic one is that she does not use footnotes or precise references (for example, page numbers) or quotations. She includes a list of works entitled "Selected Bibliography and Further Reading" at the end of the book, although it is not comprehensive, as we discovered tracking down the references for the three works that she cited in this excerpt (which we have presented as a Works Cited list). What are the advantages and disadvantages of using footnotes and explicit citations from a writer's point of view? A reader's? A publisher's?

   Answers will vary, but we suggest a few possibilities. Leaving out explicit citations is better for writers and publishers in that they don't require extreme precision or require extra pages (which can be costly); readers might appreciate the uncluttered text and the list of resources that they might actually consult rather than an intimidating list of sources. The inclusion of footnotes, however, can build the ethos of both author and publisher, and footnotes allow readers to track down exact sources of information.

   How does the absence of footnotes and explicit citations influence your evaluation of her text? Does it make it less formal and more inviting? Does it weaken Royte's ethos as a credible, trustworthy author? Why?

Answers will vary.

5. Writing assignment

Classroom Exercise: focus on the world

Count how many bottles of water, disposable or reusable, are in your classroom on the day that you discuss this piece. Also count how many are in your office, car, or home and share that with the class, and ask your students to do the same. To what degree does the presence of bottled water simply represent part of American consumerism? (You might, for example, ask students to count something else in their homes—how many spoons or sweaters do they have? Do they really need them all?) Is bottled water something that they have good reasons to buy? Ask them to write a short evaluative essay defending bottled water.

Cook's Country Magazine *Ready-to-Bake Chocolate Chip Cookies*

Cook's Illustrated Magazine *Solving the Mystery of the Chewy Chocolate Chip Cookie* pp. 843–48

1. What kind of argument is the first section of "Ready-to-Bake Chocolate Chip Cookies"? (For example, an argument of fact or of definition?) The list of recommended products?

   Both sections are heavily evaluative, but they also contain some causal arguments (e.g., adding more chips will make homemade cookies better), and the suggestion that one can bake better cookies cheaper and without preservatives could be read as a proposal argument.

   What kind of argument is "Solving the Mystery of the Chewy Chocolate Chip Cookie"? The recipe? What evidence can you provide for your claims?

   "Solving the Mystery" is largely a definition argument in which the authors establish the criteria for a certain type of cookie that they want to produce. "The Solution" section of the article is mostly a causal argument. The recipe itself

might be seen as a proposal argument or perhaps a causal argument.

2. Examine carefully the first section of "Ready-to-Bake Chocolate Chip Cookies" and the first section of "Thick and Chewy Chocolate Chip Cookies." What sorts of ethical appeals do you find in each?

   Possibilities: the authors' description of their scientific rigor or the citation of Shirley Corriher, a food scientist, as a source.

   What sorts of appeal to emotion?

   Possibilities: the authors' references to saving money and avoiding artificial ingredients might be considered emotional appeals, as they're focusing on values that the audience holds.

   To facts and reason? (For a discussion of kinds of appeals, see Chapters 2, 3, and 4.)

   Possibilities: the scientific explanation of what makes good cookies or the precise instructions in the recipes.

3–4. **Answers will vary, as will the quality of any cookies the students might bake. But you should still require them to share some cookies with you, explaining that it strengthens their ethos. (Overall, *Cook's Illustrated* generally targets serious home cooks who are interested in challenging recipes and precise instructions. *Cook's Country* targets home cooks who prefer more traditional food, and though some of their recipes can be challenging, this magazine often emphasizes quicker and easier recipes than does *Cook's Illustrated*.)**

5. Writing assignment

Classroom Exercise: focus on rhetoric

Given that there's no accounting for personal tastes, how do we make arguments about food and drink? Whose authority do you trust when it comes to judging the quality of food? What knowledge, skills, experience, or charisma makes someone trustworthy on the issue of what makes food good? Are there considerations beyond a good palate? Is it worth it to try to "educate" one's palate to learn to appreciate a wider variety of foods and flavors? Are acquired tastes worth acquiring? Why or why not?

Wrap-up Exercises for "Why Worry about Food and Water?"

1. Kathy Freston's article presents vegetarianism as important for environmental reasons; the *Cook's Illustrated* recipe for chocolate chip cookies emphasizes aesthetic appeals, including taste, to the exclusion of almost everything else. Using a Rogerian approach, write an essay in which you argue for a particular approach to thinking about how we should eat. For example, should we think most about food as a social experience, or about calorie count, cost, ease of acquisition, or nutritional value (however you define "nutritional value")? You might try experimenting with making an argument that you don't feel entirely convinced is true just to gain practice thinking about how to use evidence. Be sure to make it clear who your intended audience is.

2. Record everything that you eat and drink for one, two, or three days; then write an essay that explores some aspect of your consumption. For example, you could write about how much food you consumed that you or someone you know prepared versus how much you ate that was prepared in restaurants or factories. You could examine the distance traveled by the foods you ate, as far as you can determine. Perhaps recording what food you eat will encourage you to begin an experiment, such as trying to eat all local food, all vegan food, or all fast food—in short, you might try eating differently from your normal routine. Prepare an essay about your experience of paying more attention than usual to what you eat and drink.

3. Choose one reading from this chapter that you think makes the best case for teaching us how to think about food and water, and choose a few readings that you think do not provide as strong a case for how we should think about food. Write an evaluation argument for why the reading you chose presents the strongest case, and be careful to articulate your criteria clearly.

CHAPTER 25

What Role Should Religion Play in Public Life?

Arguing about beliefs invites us to consider both the positions that others take (and the positions we might hold) and the ways in which arguments about values are constructed. Further, the practice of argument prompts us to reflect on how people construct themselves as individuals and as members of a larger society. If you've ever spent time in another country, even another English-speaking one, you'll realize that different countries define the notion of "individual" and "member of our society" in different ways. One of the ways in which individuals and societies define themselves is through arguing about religious beliefs and ideologies. Arguing about religious beliefs provides the occasion for us to examine who we are, who we aren't, and who we aspire to be. Such reflection ultimately forces us to ask difficult questions about argument in the United States:

- Is it possible to argue publicly about fiercely held beliefs in a pluralistic society? Must such arguments end up as shouting matches, or are there alternatives? When, if ever, are shouting matches warranted? When, if ever, might alternatives prove useful? Should the goal of arguments about beliefs be winning or something else? Why?
- Is freedom of religion in the United States little more than freedom from religious discourse, at least as far as the public arena is concerned? Are there ways to permit people of faith to honor their beliefs while respecting the rights of others (either those of other faiths or those who claim no faith at all), or should public discourse seek to avoid any mention of faith?
- Are there only two sides to every argument? What is gained or lost if we acknowledge that reality is always more complex than any dichotomies we might propose?

Pew Global Attitudes Project *When It Comes to Religion, the United States Is an Outlier* pp. 851–57

1. Did any of the results of this survey surprise you? Which ones? Why? Do the findings reported for countries that you are familiar with, most notably the United States, seem reasonable? If not, what does that fact teach us about the relationship between everyday opinion and claims that are based on reliable research?

   Answers will vary, but students who do not believe the findings are reasonable expect that their experience is normative, even if it is not.

2. What factors, in your opinion, might account for why the United States is such an outlier among Western and economically advanced countries?

   Answers will vary: some might point to the country's history as a beacon of religious freedom, while other students might believe that greater religious practice in the United States is a sign of good morals. Whatever factors they cite, press students to provide reasons for their claims.

3. How do the graphs and tables in this selection contribute to the argument being made? How clear are they? How apparent are the arguments they make? Which one is easiest to understand? Which one is the most complex? Why?

   Answers will vary; one possibility is that the graphs make it easier for readers to make direct comparisons between countries.

4–5. Writing assignments

Classroom Exercise: focus on research

Choose two countries from the study that had significantly different responses but are located in a similar region (some pairs might include Jordan and Lebanon, Argentina and Brazil, India and Pakistan). Research each country's religious history, and create an argument for why the two countries offered such disparate responses to the survey. What are their most significant similarities and differences? What factors besides income influence their religious leanings?

Laurie Goodstein *More Religion, but Not the Old-Time Kind* pp. 858–63

1. How would you characterize Laurie Goodstein's argument in this selection?

   Goodstein's argument is that there is currently a surge in religious activity around the world but that it does not have the trappings of fundamentalism that were present in the past.

   Why might it be important to contextualize her subject—religion as a "rising force"—globally?

   Understanding the influence of religion globally means taking into account many different religious and political situations all over the world.

   How would you characterize the ethos Goodstein creates in discussing this topic? Why might she do so? (For a discussion of how writers create their ethos and why it's important, see Chapter 3.)

   Answers will vary.

2. Like many complex arguments, this selection contains arguments of several kinds, including definitional arguments. Based on the information given in this selection, how would you define and distinguish among the categories "fundamentalists," "evangelicals," and "Pentecostals?"

   Goodstein characterizes fundamentalists as focusing on doctrine and inerrancy. She states that evangelicals participate in revival meetings and attend seminaries, but she does not give a clear picture of evangelicals. She describes Pentecostals as putting much importance on "spirit-filled worship," speaking in tongues, and miracle healings.

   Are these definitions adequate for this context—that is, for understanding the information presented in this selection? Why or why not? (For a discussion of definitional arguments, see Chapter 9.)

   Answers will vary.

3. This selection also offers a number of causal claims. List three. What sorts of causal claims are they? Who makes the claims you've listed—the author or the sources she cites?

Answers will vary.

Is the origin of the claims important in how you or other readers might evaluate the strength or validity of the selection's arguments? Why or why not?

The origins of the claims are important because the reader will be evaluating them in an effort to gauge the credibility of the author.

How do these causal claims advance its argument(s)? (For a discussion of causal arguments, see Chapter 11.)

Answers will vary.

4. This selection contains a visual argument—a complex set of "country profiles" that provide several kinds of information about Nigeria, India, Indonesia, and Brazil—reproduced from the original version of the article. What do the profiles contribute to the selection? (In other words, do you think you would have read or understood the selection differently had this visual argument not been included? How so?) Study the information given in the country profiles. Make a list of the kinds of information each profile gives. Why is this information useful and appropriate, given the focus of the selection?

   Each country profile adds to the reader's understanding of religious growth around the world. The profiles include the number of members and the percentage of growth of groups such as Christians (Protestants, Anglicans, Catholics), Muslims, Animists, Hindus, Independents, New Religionists, and Spiritists, according to the religions that are represented in each country. This information is useful in visualizing the growth of religion around the world.

   What functions do the circles of different sizes play in communicating information? How do the photographs contribute to this visual argument?

   The circles of different sizes show the relative size of the religious community without using percentages. The photographs give a concise view of religion around the world and create a context for the article.

5. Create two country profiles like the ones given , one for the United States and one for another country of your choosing (other than the four given here). Be sure to include the sources of your information. When you have completed this assignment, compare your profile for the United States with those created by two classmates. If there are differences, seek to locate the cause(s) of those differences. For example, did you rely on different sources for the basic information you used, or did you classify, combine, or represent the information you found in different ways?

   Answers will vary.

6. Writing assignment

Classroom Exercise: focus on the argument

Are students surprised to hear that the modern world is becoming more religious? What current world events might be influencing such independent movements? How many students in the class are involved in religious organizations? Do students think that college students are more or less likely than other populations to be active in this way? Is age a factor? Is academic education a factor? What do students think about evangelization on campus? What do they think might be the best way to reach students with a spiritual or religious message? (A discussion on these questions would lead nicely into the next reading.)

D. Michael Lindsay *Evangelicalism Rebounds in Academe* pp. 865–69

1. What is Lindsay's argument?

   He argues that evangelicalism is growing in prominence and importance on college campuses.

   What sorts of evidence does Lindsay cite to support his claims?

   He cites statistical evidence, interviews, and personal observations about trends among students and faculty.

   Why is it not surprising that Lindsay relies heavily on logical arguments (that is, facts and reason) rather than, say, emotional arguments to examine a potentially controversial topic like religion on college campuses? (For a discussion of kinds of evidence, see Chapter 16; for a discussion of logical arguments, see Chapter 4.)

Religion is a subject that can be very personal for many people, so Lindsay opts for logical arguments to avoid becoming too controversial.

2. A stereotype of evangelicals (and people of faith in general) is that they are anti-intellectual, an issue that Lindsay addresses in paragraph 8. How does Lindsay counter this stereotype in that paragraph?

   He discusses the long history of Christian churches supporting learning and intellectual activity.

   How does he seek to counter it throughout the remainder of the article?

   He quotes the scholar Stanley Fish predicting that religion will be the subject that inspires the most intellectual energy in the near future, discusses a number of important scholars who are evangelicals, and analyzes what effect evangelical academics have had on college campuses already.

3. Interestingly, Lindsay does not offer readers an explicit definition of *evangelicals* in this article. At the same time, the article's statements about evangelicals—both who they are and who they aren't—can help us to assemble a definition. First, consider why Lindsay might not have included an explicit definition of the category of people that he is discussing. What are the advantages and disadvantages of not offering explicit definitions in cases like this?

   If Lindsay offered a specific definition, some readers might feel that he excluded certain types of religious people. However, by not offering a specific definition, he runs a serious risk of not communicating with his audience—they may not understand how he is using terminology.

   Second, based on the information in the article, put together a definition of the term *evangelicals* as Lindsay uses it. Finally, compare your definition with those on sites like dictionary.com. How is it similar? How is it different? (For a discussion of arguments of definition, see Chapter 9.)

   Answers may vary.

4. Lindsay's article can be analyzed as a causal argument or perhaps more accurately as a series of such arguments. Make a list of the

causal arguments that you find in this selection, and then analyze them according to the discussion "Understanding Causal Arguments" in Chapter 11.

Causal arguments: 1) What is causing the increase in evangelicals on campuses? 2) What effects will this increase have on American higher education? 3) Will evangelicals radically reshape American colleges and universities?

Analyses of these arguments may vary.

You'll see that Lindsay frequently marks the beginning of a new causal argument syntactically—that is, by use of a specific sentence form. What sentence form does he use?

Questions.

5. Lindsay's intended audience for this essay is people involved directly in higher education across the United States, administrators and faculty, in particular. Consider the audience that Lindsay invokes—that is, directly addresses or represents—in the text. What values does Lindsay expect these readers might have? Do you think that he expects them to believe in any faith? To be evangelicals? Why or why not?

   Answers may vary, but we believe that Lindsay is not addressing evangelicals; instead, he seems to be addressing people who either have little faith or who do not see faith as central to their identity in the way that evangelicals likely would.

   If you find this question challenging, you may wish to ask yourself why Lindsay ends the essay as he does. In other words, why might the topics in the last four paragraphs be placed where they are?

   Answers may vary, but we see the ending as at least partly an attempt to assuage the fears of an audience who finds the idea of evangelicals in academe threatening.

   In what ways do these paragraphs represent emotional arguments as well as logical arguments? (For a discussion of invoked audience, see Chapter 1; for a discussion of emotional arguments, see Chapter 2.)

   One good example of an emotional argument in the last few paragraphs is Lindsay's suggestion that "we can learn from

them," where he means to build a bridge between evangelicals and higher education administration and faculty.

6. Writing assignment

Classroom Exercise: focus on the world

What is the status of religious belief and expression on your campus? Are evangelicals a prominent force? What is the status of minority religions? Are religious organizations active and visible? Is religion something that students tend to keep personal and private, or is it part of the intellectual energy on your campus?

Michelle Bryant *Selling Safe Sex in Public Schools* pp. 872–75

1. What sort of ethos does Shelby Knox create for herself during the interview reported here? What role(s) does her faith play in that ethos?

   Knox creates an ethos of credibility because she is a young Christian woman who is not sexually active and who contends that sex education is the only way to provide important information to other young people.

   Would her narrative or ethos be different if Knox were an atheist? Why or why not? (For a discussion of ethos, see Chapter 3.)

   If Knox were an atheist, we might not be as surprised by her stance, and her argument would not resonate as strongly with the audience.

2. What causal arguments do you find in the narrative of Shelby Knox's experiences?

   Knox contends that by not teaching youth about safe sex, schools are contributing to unwanted pregnancies and sexually transmitted diseases. She also argues that the Lubbock Youth Commission's sex education campaign was a major factor in reducing STDs and teen pregnancy in Lubbock, Texas.

   Why are these arguments crucial to the argument made by the selection? (For a discussion of causal arguments, see Chapter 11.)

These causal arguments support Knox's larger argument that sex education is necessary for teens.

3. In paragraph 15, Knox contends, "I think that God wants you to question." What does Knox want people of faith to question? Why?

   Knox wants people to question religious tenets that call for people to turn their backs on people in need—such as sexually active teens who are confused and gay students who feel the effects of discrimination. She argues that "God loves everyone," and that as a Christian she should work to serve those in need.

   Why do you imagine Knox believes "he [God] can't use blind followers"? (Obviously, Knox is using "blind" metaphorically in this case.)

   Followers who do not think for themselves risk contradicting their own beliefs and missing opportunities to be of use to humanity.

4. This article first appeared in *Life & Letters: A Publication of the College of Liberal Arts of the University of Texas at Austin*, a magazine that highlights the research and achievements of faculty and students in the college. It's distributed within the college and to its friends and supporters, including donors, many of whom would be politically conservative and would identify as evangelical Christians. How can you see awareness of the magazine's intended audience in the selection of Shelby Knox as the topic of an article? In the way her story is presented?

   The article takes a respectful tone and does not directly criticize the local government or Christians for their beliefs. Knox's story is told factually, and any criticisms are quotes from Knox herself.

   How might the selection challenge readers holding various political or religious beliefs? How does the illustration on p. 875, which was published with the article in *Life of Letters*, contribute to the argument?

   Knox's position may be in opposition to many of the readers of the magazine, and her arguments might challenge some of their deeply held beliefs. The picture from the article shows a young woman who appears professional and

clean-cut. Her family is pictured with both parents. Her father is wearing an American flag shirt, which reiterates her family's traditional values.

5. Writing assignment

Classroom Exercise: focus on the argument

Both sides of the sexual education controversy claim to have scientific evidence that a particular program (abstinence only or safe sex) significantly influences the occurrence of sexually transmitted diseases and unwanted pregnancies. Why might this topic be controversial? What suggestions do students have for helping to avoid emotional responses to the issue? How do race, class, and religion affect the discussion? If parents are unwilling or unable to discuss safe sex with their children, who, if anyone, should be available to guide students with questions?

Melanie Springer Mock *Separation of Church and State: A War on Christmas and Other Misguided Notions* pp. 877–79

1. What stance does Mock, as a Christian, take on the issue of "the war on Christmas"?

   Mock believes that it is ridiculous to worry about the idea that there is a "war on Christmas" when one should instead focus on celebrating the season according to one's beliefs and appreciating the separation of church and state.

   What makes her stance unusual among some Christians?

   Some Christians believe that everyone should be reminded of the "reason for the season," the religious origins of the Christmas holiday.

   How does she use that fact strategically in organizing her argument?

   Perhaps Mock's most strategic move is to suggest that anyone who needs the government to put "baby Jesus on the courthouse steps to remind them of his birth" has a weak faith. Mock is strategically positioning herself as potentially more faithful than those who argue for public display of Nativity scenes.

2. What is Mock's understanding of the notion of the separation of church and state?

   Mock believes strongly that church and state should be separated and that government should be very careful not to seem to endorse any religion. Her conviction of the importance of separation of church and state derives largely from her belief that not endorsing a particular religion protects religion from government interference.

   How well does she explain it? How well does she justify it?

   Answers may vary.

3. Note the ethical appeals that Mock uses to support her position. How does she create an ethos as a Christian?

   Mock mentions how much she enjoys Christmas Eve services in the first paragraph, and at the end she talks about not needing a public reminder to feel her faith deeply. Further, throughout the essay she is proud to mention her devout faith and uses terminology such as "the Prince of Peace" easily.

   As a Mennonite?

   Mock refers to her denomination's history of being persecuted, even using the word "martyrdom" (which aligns the Mennonites with the martyrdom of Jesus) to describe their historical position.

   As an American? (For a discussion of ethical appeals and arguments, see Chapter 3.)

   Mock endorses a close adherence to the language of the First Amendment, proclaims her belief in the importance of separation of church and state, and appeals near the end of the article to the importance of the protections provided by the Constitution.

4. What sorts of emotional and logical arguments does Mock use?

   Answers may vary. Some possibilities for logical arguments include Mock's appeal to the Constitution's separation of church and state and her artistic proof that aligns public Nativity scenes with evangelism. Some possibilities for

emotional arguments include her claim that those who need public reminders of "the reason for the season" perhaps do not have enough faith and her mention that no minority faith has to face the threat of being evangelized by those in the majority.

How effective are they? (For a discussion of emotional and logical arguments, see Chapters 2 and 4, respectively.)

Answers may vary.

5. In what senses is Mock's argument a proposal? A proposal addressed specifically to Christians?

   To Christians Mock proposes not focusing on public displays but on private dedication and devotions.

   To all Americans? (For a discussion of proposal arguments, see Chapter 12.)

   To all Americans she proposes that we keep church and state well separated by not supporting government displays or endorsements of religion.

6. Writing assignment

Classroom Exercise: focus on the argument

Consider Mock's rhetorical strategies and how they might be received by different audiences. To what extent does Mock use Rogerian argument? Does she treat those with whom she disagrees fairly? Who is most likely to reject her argument? What strategies do you think that she could employ to make her argument more effective? Choose two or three different audiences and address how Mock might improve her argument with those audiences.

Antonin Scalia *God's Justice and Ours* pp. 881–86

1. Justice Scalia devotes the first part of this article to distinguishing between those who read the Constitution as a "living document," the meaning of which changes as society "matures," and those who see it as "enduring," with a focus on its meaning at the time it was drafted. What, for Scalia, are the characteristics and consequences of each view?

Those who view the Constitution as a living document believe that Supreme Court decisions must take into account our current conceptions of morality and decency and that therefore our interpretations of the Constitution evolve throughout time. Those who view the Constitution as enduring believe that justices must judge cases based on the definitions implied when the Constitution was written; their boundaries of morality and legality exist today unless modified by the legislative branch of the government.

Which of the two views do you prefer? Why? Does either one leave you uncomfortable? Why or why not?

Answers will vary.

2. Throughout the article, Scalia makes other important distinctions: cases in which the state (that is, the government) decrees death versus those where it does not restrain death from occurring (paragraph 5), private morality versus governmental morality (paragraph 10), European versus American attitudes toward religion in public life (paragraph 14), legal versus moral matters (paragraph 17), and Christian versus post-Freudian secularist perspectives on death (paragraph 15), among others. Choose two such distinctions, and specify the basis of the distinction (in each case, a kind of definition—see Chapter 9).

   Answers will vary. For one example, Scalia notes that while for post-Freudian secularists death is the end of existence and thus a cataclysmic punishment, for Christians death leads to the next phase of existence and thus is not the literal end of the world.

3. Scalia concludes by claiming that it is a good thing for American Catholics (and, by extension, people of any faith in America) to be involved in aspects of public and political life in the United States. Do you agree or disagree? Why?

   Answers will vary.

4. Scalia argues that a justice who finds the death penalty immoral should resign from the bench (paragraph 8). Do you agree or disagree? Why? Whatever your stance, you'll need to do your best to anticipate and acknowledge potential rebuttals against your position.

Answers will vary.

5. Writing assignment

Classroom Exercise: focus on the argument

Justice Scalia's comparison of religion in the United States with that in Europe corroborates the conclusions reached in the second reading of this chapter, the Pew Global Attitudes Project's report, "When It Comes to Religion, the United States Is an Outlier" (pp. 851–857). Each uses significantly different sources of evidence to draw and present conclusions. Using Chapter 16, "What Counts as Evidence," as a guide, analyze the types of evidence each uses and how they contribute to the author's argument. Consider as well which lines of argument (ethos, pathos, and logos) each reading employs and why.

Mariam Rahmani *Wearing a Head Scarf Is My Choice as a Muslim; Please Respect It* pp. 888–90

1. What is Mariam Rahmani's argument? How does she define the meaning of wearing the *hijab* and justify it?

   Rahmani's argument is that women should have the right to wear a *hijab* if they choose to. She defines wearing a *hijab* as a self-reminder to focus on developing her inner self rather than her outer self.

   How effectively does she anticipate and respond to potential counterarguments?

   Answers will vary.

2. How does Rahmani call into question Western notions of "liberation" for women?

   She dismisses Western notions of liberation for women as having resulted in objectification and pressure to be beautiful. Rahmani argues that Western-style liberation is not necessarily a positive for women.

3. If women of any faith or no faith at all believe that they're regarded by men or society at large for their "physicality," should they have to take action, or should men or society change? Why? How?

   Answers will vary.

4. Rahmani sets up a strong contrast between the West and Islam, yet she is, based on available evidence, a Muslim in and of the West. If we assume this statement is true, has Rahmani contradicted herself or weakened her argument? In other words, must there be a strong contrast between Islam and the West? Why or why not?

   Answers will vary.

5. In paragraph 13, Rahmani contends that we must "agree to disagree." Do you agree with her position, or are there alternatives she hasn't mentioned? What might they be?

   Answers will vary.

6. Writing assignment

Classroom Exercise: focus on the argument

A common argument against *hijabs* and other veils is the value of assimilation within a secular society. Many non-Muslims argue that the veil creates a barrier between Western cultures and the women and families of Islam. How might the veil create a social distance? Who should have to bear the burden of change in a situation such as this? Is assimilation the best answer? How does this question of *hijabs* compare to the wearing of yarmulkes, crosses, sacred medals, and other religious icons? At what point, if any, does a religious garment or adornment separate a person from other people?

Randy Cohen *Between the Sexes* pp. 892–93

1. Do you agree or disagree with Randy Cohen's analysis of the situation that J.L. describes? In other words, did the Orthodox Jew's refusal to shake hands with a woman who wasn't a relative by blood or marriage constitute an act of sexism in terms of the intentions of the real-estate agent or its effect upon his client? Should J.L., as Cohen suggests, have torn up the contract? Why or why not?

   Answers will vary.

2. Evaluate the responses to Cohen's column. What sorts of arguments— emotional, ethical, or logical—do the letter writers use?

   Answers will vary but may include the following examples. Cara Weinstein Rosenthal uses an argument based on character when she defines herself as "a Jew, a feminist and a fu-

ture rabbi." In addition, she makes an argument based on facts and reason when she defines the strictures of "shomer negiah" to show how they don't fit Cohen's assessment. Robert M. Gottesman uses an argument based on values when he notes that "Religious freedom is a constitutional and moral right." Helen Pogrin uses an argument from the heart when she argues that the real estate agent's refusal to shake hands was "out of respect to his own wife and to other women."

Which specific arguments do you find most persuasive? Why? (For a discussion of emotional, ethical, and logical arguments, see Chapters 2, 3, and 4, respectively.)

Answers will vary.

3. Writing assignment

Classroom Exercise: focus on the argument

Who is Randy Cohen, and why do we trust his ethical advice? Conduct research as a class to find out about his background, his credentials, and his writing and publishing history. How did he come to be "The Ethicist"? How does his title, rather than his name, function as an argument about ethos? How does your knowledge of him as a person affect your trust in his advice? Read some of his other columns, and discuss his advice. Do you frequently agree with him? Do you disagree? What are the main issues on which your opinion differs from Cohen's?

This I Believe

Albert Einstein *An Ideal of Service to Our Fellow Man* pp. 895–97

Eboo Patel *We Are Each Other's Business* pp. 897–98

Penn Jillette *There Is No God* pp. 898–99

1. Which of these three arguments do you find the most effective? Why? Seeking to put aside whatever religious beliefs you might have, which writer do you think makes the strongest case for his beliefs? Why?

   Answers will vary.

2. Choose the essay that you believe is strongest, and characterize it. Is it an argument of fact? Of definition? Of evaluation? Is it causal? Is it a proposal? What role does religious belief—or the lack of it—play in structuring the argument?

   Answers will vary. Einstein's essay might be seen as a proposal argument, as it ends with his recommendation for "a planned economy coupled with an education geared toward social goals." Patel's essay might also be a proposal argument, encouraging his audience to act on the idea of pluralism. Jillette's essay might be seen as a causal argument, detailing the effects of embracing atheism.

3. How is the essay by Einstein like the essays by Patel and Jillette? How is it different? In considering this question, pay attention to all aspects of the essays, but especially language, formality, the ways in which personal experiences are used, and the ways in which personal beliefs are expressed. What might account for the differences?

   Answers will vary, but let us mention a couple of points of difference. Einstein's essay is more formal and directed toward explaining a vision of society, while both Patel and Jillette emphasize their personal opinions and experiences. Both Patel and Jillette, fittingly, begin their essays with the word "I". A difference in social roles could explain the differences. Einstein was a public intellectual who could speak about how things ought to be, while Patel and Jillette, though public figures, do not have the stature that Einstein did. The differences might also be generational: perhaps there is a more modern trend of speaking about religion more personally?

4–5. Writing assignments

Classroom Exercise: focus on the world

(This exercise is a way to expand upon question 5 in the Respond section.) Take the essay that you wrote for the *This I Believe* series and reframe your approach. If you wrote a straightforward, thesis-driven essay that states your beliefs, try recasting your argument as a narrative—tell a story that illustrates your opinion. If you wrote a narrative argument the first time around, try rewriting your story as a claim-driven essay. Which one do you think would be more effective for a radio audience? Why?

Wrap-up Exercises for "What Role Should Religion Play in Public Life?"

These three activities are suggested as wrap-up exercises in which students integrate any or all of the readings of the chapter. In addition, exercises 1 and 2 would be suitable for an in-class essay assignment.

1. Construct an argument for the use of violence as an appropriate response to particular issues. The violence could be symbolic (for example, shouting a speaker down, not permitting certain subjects to be discussed publicly) or real (for example, responding with physical violence). In your essay, you will need to delimit clearly the circumstances under which you contend a violent response is justified and the nature of the violent response that you believe to be justifiable. You will also need to assess the consequences for all involved—the one(s) silenced or attacked, the silencer(s) or attacker(s), and society at large (especially because our society permits freedom of expression but acknowledges that its members hold a range of opinions on most issues).

2. Write an essay in which you delimit the boundaries of either freedom of expression or freedom of religion in this society. Be sure to provide justifications for any boundaries you set and discuss the consequences of accepting them for individuals and for society at large. If you contend that there should be no boundaries on freedom of expression or religion, justify your position by describing how to resolve conflicts that might arise with respect to the expression of ideas (or manner of their expression) or of religious beliefs. (One way to approach these subjects may be to ask yourself whether there are certain topics or ways of arguing that should not be permitted in this society or whether there are certain ritual practices that should not be permitted in the name of religion. Infant sacrifice, for example, would likely be an example of the latter for all Americans, though the practice occurred in times past in certain societies.)

3. Rewrite one of the arguments you've written for this course that required you to take an explicit stance on a particular issue. If the original argument was primarily agonistic, the rewritten essay

should be invitational. If the original argument was primarily invitational, the new version should be agonistic. As you'll discover, this assignment is more complex than it might appear at first glance. Such revisions typically require not only a shift in tone but also changes with respect to the kinds of support used and even the statement of the thesis itself.

CHAPTER 26

What Should "Diversity on Campus" Mean?

Because we believe that all people are equal, colleges and universities strive to include students of diverse backgrounds to ensure that one group of people is not dominating the educated class. Equally important, schools seek diversity to enrich the learning environment by bringing a multiplicity of voices and experiences to campus. But what if certain ideologies take hold of academia? What if we have been misreading the effects of diversity or have an overly limited understanding of what constitutes diversity? And how real is purposeful, calculated diversity? The readings in this cluster invite us to consider what problems need to be fixed and what actions should be taken to fix them. This consideration leads us to ask the following questions:

- What constitutes true diversity? How do we measure diversity? What determining characteristics of identity allow us to measure diversity?
- Should educational institutions be representative of the city, state, or U.S. population in race? Gender? Political ideology? Religion? What characteristics are the most important to balance? Why?
- Schools still talk about diversity and affirmative action, but there is a large movement to remove any preferential admission or hiring programs for minorities of any type. What are the disadvantages of these programs? What alternatives are there to affirmative action programs?

Making a Visual Argument: Student-Designed Diversity Posters

Joseph Wagner *Peeling Off Labels*

Stephanie Heyman *Everyone a Part, No One Apart*

Melanie Frost *Embracing Diversity in University Residences*

Hannah Leimback *Identities Are Infinite . . . What's Yours?*

Megan Stampfli *Embrace Diversity* pp. 903–7

1. Which of these visual arguments do you find most appealing? Least appealing? Why?

   Answers will vary.

2. Analyze the relationship between text (the words used) and the visual images and layout in each of the posters. What's the interaction between the text, on the one hand, and the visual images and layout, on the other, in each one?

   "Identities Are Infinite . . ." uses words to display multiple possibilities for identity. "Embrace Diversity" uses words in collage form mixed over a picture to finish the sentence "Diversity Is . . ."

   Which poster is most effective in this regard? Why?

   Answers will vary.

3. If you take each of these posters to be a definitional argument, defining diversity in some way, what argument is each making? In other words, how does each poster define *diversity*? (For a discussion of definitional arguments, see Chapter 9.)

   The posters define diversity as the many parts of one whole, the many aspects of identity that we all have, tapestry, the absence of bias, the acceptance of others, and seeing beyond stereotypes.

4. In defining and commenting on the notion of diversity, these posters range from approaching the topic in a didactic fashion (that is, seeking to teach a moral lesson) to approaching it much more vaguely. (Note the evaluative—and potentially negative—connotations the labels "didactic" and "vague" carry.) Choose the posters that you find most explicitly didactic and those that you find most vague in their approach to the topic. Justify your choices. Which approach do you prefer? Why? Which do you believe is more effective in situations like this one? Why?

   Answers will vary.

5–6. Writing assignments

Classroom Exercise: focus on rhetoric

Having evaluated the different posters by answering the questions at the end of the chapter, students should be aware of what they thought was effective and what wasn't. Have students create a "call for posters" that announces a poster contest at their own school. They should include a list of requirements or tips for a quality poster that will draw student attention. Students should share their requirements with the class and discuss their own experiences with school-sponsored public service ads (they might be memorable ones, inappropriate ones, ridiculous ones, and so on).

Sarah Karnasiewicz *The Campus Crusade for Guys* pp. 909–15

1. What argument(s) is Karnasiewicz making with respect to the nature of diversity on campus?

   Karnasiewicz is arguing that many colleges are seeing an increase in the proportion of females to males.

   How persuasive do you find it? Why? Should there be affirmative action for men? Why or why not?

   Answers will vary.

2. Although this article is about gender, it's also about issues of race, ethnicity, and class as well as the intersection of these social variables. What sorts of observations or claims are made about each of these variables in the article?

   The crusade for boys is similar to affirmative action for minorities at the university level. Like affirmative action, some pundits argue that preparing boys for college needs to start in elementary education. The author also points out that the disproportionate achievement of boys is even stronger at lower socioeconomic levels. If schools are failing young men, then we certainly need to look at the poorest school districts.

   Do you agree or disagree with them? Do you find any of the claims made about these topics troubling? Why or why not?

Answers will vary.

3. How and why are females and males stigmatized by a lack of education or by the kind of job they might hold?

   Uneducated women tend to hold lower-paying jobs than uneducated men do. Those men are more likely to be in skilled-labor positions while women are in service industries. As the author notes, women can be stigmatized for having too much education, and while pundits discuss a possible "dearth" of educated men for these educated women to marry, no one was concerned that men would not have educated partners back when they were the larger school population.

   Although it isn't mentioned, in what ways might the marriage market encourage young women to attend college (or even to succeed academically, more broadly)?

   College is a good place to meet an educated husband. On the other hand, if women want to prepare themselves to be self-sufficient in case marriage does not work out for them, college also provides good training.

4. What's the allusion in Karnasiewicz's title? (If you need a hint, check out http://ccci.org.) How and why is it appropriate, given the subject matter of the article?

   The Campus Crusade for Christ is a national Christian organization for university students. The club name is generally well known on campuses, and the title of this article takes advantage of that name recognition.

   Is the allusion risky in any way? Why or why not?

   This play on words is witty, but it may offend some students.

5. Among the kinds of evidence that Karnasiewicz uses effectively is statistics. Where and how do she and those she cites use statistics advantageously?

   The author and those she cites use statistics to show how many schools have far more men than women. We don't see numbers for schools that have equal numbers of men and women.

In what ways does she qualify claims made on the basis of statistical data? How does qualifying arguments in this way contribute to Karnasiewicz's ethos? (For a discussion of using facts like statistics, see Chapter 4; for a discussion of ethos, see Chapter 3.)

Karnasiewicz questions whether the statistics about college men tell the whole story. Men still earn more than women, and men without a college education earn just as much as those with an education. Presenting these facts lends the author an air of evenhandedness.

6. Writing assignment

Classroom Exercise: focus on the argument

Looking around the campus, do students notice a difference in the number of males compared to the number of females? Have men in the class felt like a minority at any point? Have women noticed a general lack of men on campus? Is there a public policy about male recruitment on campus? What do students think will draw men to campus, and what lengths do they think are appropriate for their school? Is it important to maintain a minimum number of men at the university? Why? The author points out how this situation parallels affirmative action for minority students, but how might these situations be different?

Making a Visual Argument: Cartoonists Take on Affirmative Action

Mike Lester *It's GOT to Be the Shoes*

Dennis Draughon *Supreme Irony*

Mike Thompson *Daniel Lives on Detroit's Eastside . . .*

Signe Wilkinson *Admissions*

Dean Camp *Pricey* pp. 917–20

1. Briefly summarize the argument being made by each cartoon.

Lester's argument is that racial preferences allow minorities who are not prepared or perhaps qualified to enter college. The Draughon cartoon can have at least two readings: the irony that a nondiverse Supreme Court makes decisions

about diversity issues and the irony that many feel that Clarence Thomas was appointed simply to fill the seat vacated by another African American, Thurgood Marshall, even though Thomas was not as well qualified as some other candidates. Thompson argues that affirmative action helps those who have followed a difficult road to college. Wilkinson argues that many students who receive preferential treatment are not minorities. Camp suggests that wealthier students have the advantage of tutoring and other preparatory programs that others do not have access to.

Which do you find most effective? Least effective? Why?

Answers will vary.

2. In what ways do the cartoons by Mike Lester and Dennis Draughon mock the Supreme Court?

   Lester uses a clown-judge to claim that the Court is acting ridiculously to allow "unprepared students" into college through racial preference, while Draughon focuses on Justice Clarence Thomas as a member of a minority on the Court.

   How does Lester's cartoon use gender and gender stereotypes humorously? How might Sarah Karnasiewicz, author of "The Campus Crusade for Guys," respond to this cartoon?

   Boys often develop more slowly than girls, and recently it has been argued that men are not as prepared for college as women are. Karnasiewicz would probably point out that regarding preferences for men, the cartoon is right. It might not be a case of men needing help to get into college but of men choosing other paths.

   How does each of these cartoons use irony?

   Irony can be seen, respectively, as a white male enters college ahead of a female based on the precedent of racial preferences, a minority in a largely homogeneous group ponders diversity, a minority student who faces difficult odds is accused of being given too many breaks because he enters college through affirmative action, a minority is accused of bumping out a college applicant when there are four other students who might deserve to be there even

less, and a white male entering college ahead of others because of preparatory services that he paid for.

3. In what ways do the cartoons by Mike Thompson and Signe Wilkinson make similar arguments? How do their arguments differ?

   Both point out that people are often quick to claim that minorities have stolen a spot in school from a better-educated student without stopping to ponder the other circumstances involved. They differ in that the first addresses the reasoning behind affirmative action, while the other points out that privileged persons have long received special consideration for admission.

4. How can the cartoon by Dean Camp be read as relevant to debates about affirmative action?

   This cartoon can be seen as a rebuttal to the argument that minorities get all the breaks. Camp reminds the reader that students who come from high-income families (often nonminorities) have more access to courses and coaching to prepare them to compete for college admissions.

5. Writing assignment

Classroom Exercise: focus on the argument

These cartoons represent at least two different views on affirmative action. Have students choose a cartoon that they do not agree with and write a response to the artist. Encourage students to evaluate the cartoon and offer as many insights as they can about the image, text, ethos, and validity of the argument.

David Horowitz *In Defense of Intellectual Diversity* pp. 922–27

1. What argument(s) is David Horowitz making?

   Horowitz is arguing that those with conservative views are being penalized on college campuses and are in need of a bill of rights to protect them.

   How valid do you find it? Why?

   Answers will vary.

2. How does Horowitz characterize the recent history of higher education in America in paragraphs 4–5 and 10? Pay special attention to his word choices—for example, "restore academic values" in paragraph 10.

   The author states that institutions of higher education have increasingly been catering to politically correct agendas instead of focusing on education.

   How do they give you insight into his understanding of the history of higher education and the readers he's invoking? What evidence does he provide for his claims?

   The reader is able to understand that Horowitz does not believe that political views belong in the classroom. His invoked reader is someone who might have already heard negative things about the Academic Bill of Rights. His tone is that of someone defending himself. The author offers evidence in the form of incidents that occurred at Duke University and the University of North Carolina at Chapel Hill.

3. Horowitz is critical of professors who discuss "controversial matter on the war in Iraq or the Bush White House in a class whose subject matter is not the war in Iraq, or international relations, or presidential administrations," arguing that the "intrusion of such subject matter, in which the professor has no academic expertise, is a breach of professional responsibility and a violation of a student's academic rights" (paragraph 19). From Horowitz's perspective, should the arguments in Chapters 21 through 27 of this textbook be seen as breaches of the authors' professional responsibility or a violation of your academic rights? Why or why not? By what criteria can such decisions be made?

   Answers will vary.

4. Writing assignment

Classroom Exercise: focus on the argument

Have students ever had a difficulty with a professor who penalized them purely for their opinion? Do students think that a student bill of rights would protect them in these cases? Even with an explanation of rights, how do people decide whether a professor is inappropriately pushing political rhetoric versus objectively evaluating a piece of literature that addresses a topic about which they feel strongly? Who should be the arbiter in such a situation? What should constitute proof?

Stanley Fish *"Intellectual Diversity": The Trojan Horse of a Dark Design* pp. 929–34

1. What is Stanley Fish's attitude toward the Academic Bill of Rights and the notion of intellectual diversity?

   Fish states that the Academic Bill of Rights is a mistake that will politicize academia even more. He argues that while professors should not preach their ideologies in class, there should be no mandate to spend equal time in class on theories or methodologies other than their own.

   Which issues do Fish and David Horowitz, author of the Academic Bill of Rights, agree about? Which issues do they disagree about? Why?

   Both authors agree that students should be able to learn in an environment that is not made hostile by politics or religion. They disagree about the level of "diverse opinions" that should be presented on campus and the level of formal oversight that should exist to promote such diversity.

2. Fish argues that if one agrees that "the pursuit of truth is the cardinal value of the academy," then one must reject the notion of intellectual diversity (paragraph 13). What arguments does he offer for this position?

   Fish states that truths are not infallible but that this doesn't mean they must constantly be attacked.

   Do you agree or disagree? Why?

   Answers will vary.

3. In paragraphs 14–15, Fish likewise rejects the idea that the job of higher education is to produce "creative individuals" and help students become "productive citizens." What are his arguments for this position?

   Fish argues that higher education exists to train students in academics. While some character building might happen as

a result of that education, he claims that it is not the responsibility of the institution.

Do you agree or disagree? Why?

Answers will vary.

4. In paragraphs 16–23, Fish contends that despite Horowitz's claims to the contrary, his goal is to "hoist the left by its own petard." What evidence does Fish provide for his claims?

   The author points out that phrases like "intellectual diversity" and "political correctness" have been appropriated by the right.

   How do these claims compare with Horowitz's comments in his essay, "In Defense of Intellectual Diversity" (p. 922)?

   Horowitz claims that he is not plotting against the left and that he hopes that the left will embrace his Academic Bill of Rights to protect all students.

5. In paragraph 24, Fish argues that the notion of balance is an unworthy academic goal. What does he mean here?

   Here Fish uses the notion of balance to mean giving equal attention to all possible theories on a matter.

   Should the idea of balance mean that all possible positions are represented as being of equal value? Should it have some other meaning? Is it, as Fish contends, in contrast to Horowitz, not a useful goal in the pursuit of knowledge or truth?

   Answers will vary.

6. Throughout this book, we've argued that images are arguments. Let's consider the photo of Lynne Cheney that appears near the end of this selection. As the caption notes, it shows Cheney campaigning with her husband, who later served as vice president from 2001 to 2009. We can imagine some readers criticizing us for using a photo of Cheney in which she is represented as acting on behalf of her husband rather than being represented in terms of her own professional achievements. Why might such readers be critical? Others might praise us for using this photo. What might their reasoning be?

   The reference in the essay is to Lynne Cheney herself and

her political views. A photo of her with her husband might be criticized as creating an image of her as a political wife rather than as an academic and political activist in her own right. Others might counter that she has become famous through her role as the wife of the vice president and is most recognized in this role.

What is your opinion about the choice of this photo? What values led you to your conclusions?

Answers may vary.

7. Writing assignment

Classroom Exercise: focus on the argument

Stanley Fish has a fairly narrow view of the job of college professors. Do you agree? Does your school contribute to the education of your character? Has it made you more creative? Should it do either of those things? With the rest of your class, brainstorm a list of what you think your college or university should help you do and what it should not help you do. What are you expecting from your education? If a professor ventures outside academic training, how far is too far?

Patricia Cohen *Professors' Liberalism Contagious? Maybe Not* pp. 936–38

1. The first half of this article contends that an "article of faith" among certain critics of American higher education may, in fact, be false. What is the article of faith, and what arguments and evidence does Cohen cite that may undercut it?

   The article of faith is "that liberal professors politically indoctrinate their students" (paragraph 1). Cohen cites research from Fritschler, Mayer, and Smith; Woessner and Kelly-Woessner; and Mariani and Hewitt. All of these researchers say that there is no evidence of indoctrination.

2. The second half of this article takes a different turn, arguing that there is, indeed, a problem on American campuses but a problem of a very different nature. According to this section of the article, what is the real problem?

   The second half of the article suggests that the problem is "academic groupthink" on campus and that there is not

enough diversity of political opinion on the faculty or enough teaching of traditional subjects.

Cohen closes this article by indirectly quoting A. Lee Fritschler: "If anything . . . the problem is not too much politics, but too little" (paragraph 19). What does Fritschler mean by this statement?

Fritschler means that there is not enough engagement in civic and political affairs.

What would you imagine Fritschler's own political values and commitments to be? Why?

Answers may vary—be sure to press students to provide evidence for their opinions (they might, for example, look up the associations of his publisher).

3. In paragraph 15, Cohen quotes K. C. Johnson: "The conservative critics are inventing a straw man that doesn't exist and are missing the real problem that does." What does Johnson mean?

   Johnson thinks that the concern over political indoctrination is the wrong concern to have because the real problem is the loss of traditional areas of intellectual inquiry.

   What is a straw man, when one is discussing arguments?

   A straw man is an argument, weaker or more extreme than the real argument one wants to dismiss, that is created because it is easier to knock down than the real argument.

   Does it involve ethical, emotional, or logical appeals? Why?

   A straw man is usually considered a fallacy of logical argument because it fails to treat the logic of the real argument honestly.

   What is the specific straw man that Johnson contends is being created in this situation? (For a discussion of fallacies of argument, including a straw-man argument, see Chapter 17.)

   Johnson thinks that the idea that professors are indoctrinating students is the straw man because that's not the threat that he thinks really matters.

4. Cohen mentions the American Council of Trustees and Alumni (paragraph 16) and the National Association of Scholars (para-

graph 18). Do some research on these two organizations to discover their positions and the values to which they are committed. In light of this research, evaluate Anne Neal's claim that "it is not about left and right." In other words, based on your research, would you expect that most of the members of these two organizations are politically conservative and therefore affiliated with the right or politically liberal and therefore affiliated with the left? Why?

Answers may vary depending on how students interpret the evidence, but both organizations are generally recognized as politically conservative and associated with the right.

Is this information relevant to Neal's claim? Why or why not?

Answers may vary, though we tend to think it's relevant, especially if we consider professors' political views to be relevant.

5. Writing assignment

Classroom Exercise: focus on rhetoric

Cohen is careful to interview subjects who disagree in some way with the primary claim that professors indoctrinate students. Evaluate her choice of whom to interview. Is she choosing sources that you trust to have an informed opinion? Now take a look at a news source that you generally trust and evaluate how a few different stories balance the claims of opposing opinions. Do all stories need to be told from two sides? Does this tactic present any weaknesses or problems? Do you feel that the media source that you examined is generally fair in the presentation of news, or do you think that you trust them because they usually confirm things you want to hear?

Mack D. Mariani and Gordon J. Hewitt *Indoctrination U.? Faculty Ideology and Changes in Student Political Orientation* (Excerpt) pp. 941–47

1. One purpose of this research was to use the statistical analysis of data gathered from students to test a claim that is commonly made by conservative critics of American universities. What claim is being tested? State this claim as a Toulmin argument. (For a discussion of Toulmin argumentation, see Chapter 7.)

Answers may vary to some degree. We offer the following.

Claim: We should change higher education in the United States in some way (for example, Horowitz wants to add the Academic Bill of Rights while others want to hire more professors who are conservative).

Reason: Students at American colleges and universities are being indoctrinated by left-wing professors.

Warrant: Students should not be subject to political indoctrination.

Backing: Students should be allowed to think for themselves in college. Classrooms are appropriate for studying academic subjects, not for listening to professors spout off their political opinions.

2. What did Mariani and Hewitt find when they tested the claim discussed in question 1?

   They found there was little evidence that students' political views were changing over their college careers.

   What is the difference between a purely logical argument (as discussed in question 1) and one that is based on empirical data (as is the case in this research)?

   Most of all, the arguments depend on different kinds of evidence. For example, those who claim that professors indoctrinate students might be right that professors are left-wingers and that students are in vulnerable positions, but that still doesn't mean that the students will be converted by the professors. (Students might be savvy about negotiating the attempted conversion, or professors might be bad at indoctrinating.) The logical theory about how professors might be changing students doesn't provide the same information as the empirical evidence that measures actual changes.

3. Briefly outline the "Discussion" section of this selection to get a clear idea how it is structured. In outlining, you are looking for the major topic of each paragraph and the way that the paragraphs work together to conclude the article. Based on this particular "Discussion" section, how would you characterize the functions of

a discussion section of a research article? In other words, how is this section structured and why?

The "Discussion" section first summarizes the findings of the research, then considers how those data are or are not surprising, then discusses the limitations of the research, and then summarizes the most important findings. The structure lets us see what the research teaches us, acknowledges that it is not perfect, and ends with a reconsideration of what the research means and how we should think about the information.

4. A large part of the "Discussion" section describes the limitations of the research. How does this discussion contribute to the researchers' ethos? In what ways does an acknowledgment of the limitations of a research study function like qualifiers in an argument?

   The discussion of limitations enhances the authors' ethos by showing that they understand that there might be limitations to what their research can establish. The acknowledgment of limitations functions just like qualifiers in an argument because this acknowledgment places limits on the claims and the responsibilities of the arguments.

   How does the authors' note—the unnumbered footnote indicated by an asterisk—contribute to their ethos? (For a discussion of ethos, see Chapter 3. For a discussion of qualifiers, see Chapter 7.)

   This note is likely to enhance the authors' ethos greatly by suggesting that the research team does not have the goal of only supporting one side in this debate and that they have a balanced approach to the question.

5. Writing assignment

Classroom Exercise: focus on the argument

Compare this article with the previous news article that summarizes the results of several studies on faculty ideology. What features of the argument mark Mariani and Hewitt's article as academic argument? What are the strengths of academic argument on an issue like this? What are the strengths of the less academic argument presented by Cohen? Which argument do you find more compelling? Why? In what contexts and with what audiences might the argument that you find less compelling actually be more persuasive?

Libby Sander *Blue-Collar Boomers Take Work Ethic to College* pp. 949–52

1. What argument(s) is Libby Sander making in this selection?

   Sander argues that an increasing number of blue-collar workers are returning to school, usually to get better jobs.

   What factors account for the situation that she is describing?

   She focuses on returning students who are seeking work that is less physically demanding or pays more.

   To what extent are these older Americans becoming students as a matter of choice? As a matter of necessity?

   It's sometimes unclear precisely what role choice and necessity play in these decisions; necessity sounds tremendously important for some of the returning students, though many have clearly made a choice.

   As Sander describes the situation, in what ways does social class intersect with the values that these students bring to school with them?

   Her article suggests that these students who have labored at physically demanding jobs for years bring a work ethic and a no-nonsense approach that will help them in school.

2. As noted, this article was written before the economic downturn of 2008. How has the economic situation in the United States changed since that time?

   Answers to this question will vary depending on when students read this article.

   Do you believe that these changes have had any influence on who is attending college or why? What evidence might you offer for your position?

   Answers will vary.

3. What sorts of evidence does Sander present to support her claims?

Sander relies on some surveys but mostly on personal interviews.

How might her article have been different if she had relied only on, let's say, statistics?

The story would have had a much less personal tone and made fewer emotional appeals.

How would the tone of the article, for example, have been different?

Her tone might have been more academic and, arguably, drier and less interesting.

4. How does the presence of older Americans on campus change the nature of college life? How might the life experiences of people like Russell Kearney, David Cox, and Dannie Hill influence their behavior as students? How might they influence the nature or content of class discussions, for example? What advantages might there be to having a student population that is not all of a single age cohort?

   Answers will vary, but we would suggest that older students often bring more seriousness and sense of purpose to their studies; Sander's argument certainly supports that view. One advantage of a more diverse cohort of students in terms of age is that older students might bring an ability to make concrete connections between what students learn in school and how they live the rest of their lives. On the other hand, younger students might bring an enthusiasm and an ability to question that will complement the learning patterns of the older students.

5. Writing assignment

Classroom Exercise: focus on the world

Interview a few people who are older than you about their experience with higher education. If your interviewee did not go to college, does he or she regret it? What led to the choice not to attend? (Did it even feel like a choice at the time?) If your interviewee did attend, what advice would he or she give to students attending now? Share the advice that you collected with that advice collected by your other classmates. Do patterns emerge? Could you employ the advice that older people gave you about college?

Edward F. Palm *The Veterans Are Coming! The Veterans Are Coming!* pp. 955–61

1. In what ways is Palm's essay a proposal argument?

   Palm first identifies a potential problem (that campuses will not know how to handle an influx of veterans on campus) and offers specific solutions for how to solve the problem (the five pieces of advice with which he ends the article).

   What does he propose?

   He proposes five guidelines for making a campus welcoming for veterans: treat veterans like any other students; don't thank veterans for their service if you don't know them; don't shy away from political discussions in class; don't ask about their war experience but wait for them to decide if they want to speak about it; and expect veterans to succeed.

   What situation leads him to offer his proposal?

   The most immediate situation is the passage of a new GI Bill that will support the desire of many veterans to get a college education. Palm's own experience as a veteran and an academic has also influenced him to make this proposal.

   How appropriate do you find Palm's advice? (For a discussion of proposal argument, see Chapter 12.)

   Answers will vary.

2. The first half of Palm's essay is based on personal experiences. In what ways does Palm use these experiences to construct logical arguments? Ethical arguments? Emotional arguments? (For a discussion of these kinds of arguments, see Chapters 4, 3, and 2, respectively.) An interesting way to think about this question would be to consider what the essay would be like if it began with paragraph 15.

   One example of a logical argument would be Palm's argument that students who have experienced boot camp would

better appreciate the opportunity to get an education. Palm builds on his own experience as a veteran to get us to trust his knowledge of what it means to be a veteran who attends college. In writing about his youthful experiences as a Marine, and of another young man who went back home after a few weeks of boot camp, he also builds an emotional bridge by reminding readers of their own youth and how difficult it could be to make sense of life then.

3. One resource that writers and arguments have is their readers' knowledge of earlier texts, events, and situations. By referring to specific things that readers know, writers communicate more than they explicitly say. (*Intertextuality* is the technical label for this relationship, especially when it involves relationships between written texts or text-like things, such as films.) Palm takes advantage of this fact throughout this essay. How, for example, does an understanding of the allusion in the title, the poem by Kipling, the New Testament story of Paul, the *Rambo* novel and the movies it inspired, and the Roth short story strengthen and enrich Palm's argument? How does such intertexuality contribute to Palm's ethos?

   Answers will vary, but we would offer a couple of suggestions about how the stories affect his argument and his ethos. First, we would suggest that when he mentions the *Rambo* novel and movies, Palm comes across as knowledgeable about one way that popular culture imagines veterans, as driven nearly crazy by their desire for revenge. When he quotes the Kipling poem, Palm perhaps comes across as well educated, as it's not a particularly famous poem (the same might be true of the Roth story). The poem also establishes a tradition of asking people to think about veterans first and foremost as people. The mention of the road to Damascus might allow Palm to connect with more religious readers, and it establishes an understanding that joining military culture could be such an affecting event that it is like a spiritual conversion.

   What is missed by readers who do not have knowledge of these texts, events, or situations?

   Answers will vary, but they might miss out on some of the dimensions of meaning suggested in the answers to the previous questions.

4. Giving advice to others, especially people you do not know well, is always a challenging rhetorical task. How well does Palm do? Consider the tone that he uses in the final third of the essay, where he gives "five pieces of common sense advice (paragraph 20)". How would you characterize it? Do you find the tone effective? Why or why not?

   Answers will vary, but we find the tone to be fair-minded and polite while still authoritative. One piece of evidence that he is fair-minded is that he mentions that both members of the military and college administrators can be overbearing or excessively kind; that is, they do not conform to easy stereotypes. One piece of evidence that he is authoritative would be that his recommendations are directive without entertaining lots of alternative possibilities.

5–6. Writing assignments

Classroom Exercise: focus on the world

If you're not a veteran, what do you think about Palm's concern that campuses might not be veteran-friendly? Based on your experience, is there reason to have doubts about how professors and administrators might treat veterans? What about other students? If you are a veteran, what has your experience on campus been like? Do you agree with Palm's suggestions? Do you have suggestions for making your campus more welcoming to veterans?

Walter Benn Michaels *The Trouble with Diversity: How We Learned to Love Identity and Ignore Inequality* pp. 963–68

1. What, for Walter Benn Michaels, is the real issue that American society needs to confront?

   Economic inequality.

   How, for him, does defining *diversity* in terms of a celebration of difference, especially ethnic difference, prevent Americans from both seeing the real issue and doing anything about it?

   The celebration of difference means that we don't pay attention to the importance of eliminating differences such as income inequality.

In what ways does our society's focus on ethnic and cultural diversity necessarily perpetuate racism and biological essentialism (paragraph 10)?

This focus makes us believe in the idea of racial identity and related values, not allowing us to question whether there even are biological differences between different races.

2. Why and how are these issues relevant to discussions of diversity on campus in general?

   Michaels is arguing for a different way of thinking about diversity, not for discounting the value of diversity. How a campus defines diversity determines what kind of diversity it will pursue—what students it will recruit, give scholarship money to, and so forth.

   On the campus you attend?

   Answers will vary.

3. Later in this introduction, Michaels, a liberal, points out ways in which both conservatives and liberals in American public life, first, focus on racial or ethnic differences rather than issues of social inequality and, second, benefit from doing so. In a 2004 essay, "Diversity's False Solace," he notes:

   > [W]e like policies like affirmative action not so much because they solve the problem of racism but because they tell us that racism is the problem we need to solve. . . . It's not surprising that universities of the upper middle class should want their students to feel comfortable [as affirmative action programs enable and encourage them to do]. What is surprising is that diversity should have become the hallmark of liberalism.

   Analyze the argument made in this paragraph as a Toulmin argument. (For a discussion of Toulmin argumentation, see Chapter 7.)

   Answers may vary somewhat, but we offer this possibility:

   Claim: Diversity should not be the hallmark of liberalism.

   Reason: Diversity is more about making people feel good about themselves than it is about solving a problem.

Warrant: Liberals should care about solving problems, not about making people feel good about themselves.

Backing: Liberals are devoted to the common good.

4. How would you characterize Michaels's argument? In what ways is it an argument of fact?

   Michaels traces some of the history of the interest in diversity to argue for how we have come to the understanding that we have now.

   A definitional argument?

   Michaels argues that we define diversity in one particular way and he wants to offer a new definition for us to use.

   An evaluative argument?

   Michaels evaluates the current state of our pursuit of equality.

   A causal argument?

   Michaels examines why we think the way that we do today and what problems result from that way of thinking.

   A proposal? (For a discussion of these kinds of arguments, see Chapters 8–12.)

   Michaels is proposing a new way of thinking about what constitutes diversity and a new way of achieving the goal of social justice; he implies other proposal arguments about changing our institutions, too, but this introduction doesn't spell those proposals out.

5. Writing assignment

Classroom Exercise: focus on the argument

For whom is Michaels writing? Do you think that his argument will appeal to conservatives? To liberals? To libertarians? What audience do you think is his intended audience? Who is his invoked audience? What evidence can you cite for your answers to these questions? Research some of the reviews of Michaels's book that came out when the book was published or reader reviews that appear on Amazon.com or bn.com. What kind of audience is most receptive to his argument? Why?

Wrap-up Exercises for "What Should 'Diversity on Campus' Mean?"

These final assignments are provided as an opportunity to reflect on the readings as a whole and to construct arguments based on what students have taken away from the selections. Question 3 is appropriate for use as an in-class essay.

1. Investigate the diversity mission at your institution by looking at various Web sites and statistics that may be published. Then look for any news items over the years that chronicle your school's history of minority inclusion. Write an essay in which you evaluate the progress or lack of progress that you see in the school's definition of diversity and its handling of diversity.

2. Interview five to ten students at your institution about their views of the liberal or conservative nature of the school. Concentrate on interviewing individuals who probably hold different political ideals than your own to familiarize yourself with that point of view with regard to your own environment. Find out how they view the institution as a whole, as well as other students, professors, and the level of ideology in the classroom, and also uncover their ideas about remedying any problems that they see. Use what you learn to write an essay in which you evaluate their claims and present what you understand to be happening on campus.

3. Write an essay about how you would increase the cultural diversity of a student body or the ideological diversity of a faculty if you were the head of a committee charged with presenting possible tools for increasing diversity without using affirmative action. Alternatively, construct an argument for affirmative action as the best way to increase either student or faculty diversity.

CHAPTER 27

What Are You Working For?

The readings in this chapter explore how work fits into our lives and how we think we should prepare students for their working lives. Some students, of course, are deeply enmeshed in the world of work right now; for others, the world of work is something separate from their student lives, something they will only encounter once they graduate. In either case, most of these readings should not feel like an abstract discussion of issues that don't pertain to students, for they address issues that will affect every student at some point.

Some of the readings here are most concerned with making a living, but most ask questions about how our work constitutes part of ourselves. Some of the questions that the chapter raises include:

- How does work fit into a life? What portion of our time and energy should we devote to work?
- What makes work meaningful? What kinds of work are worth doing?
- How should education relate to work? What education should young people get for their working lives? What education should we be willing to pay for to prepare young people?

Dave Isay, ed. *Dr. Monica Mayer, 45, Interviewed by Her Cousin and Patient, Spencer Wilkinson, Jr., 39* pp. 972–73
Ken Kobus, 58, Tells His Friend Ron Baraff, 42, about Making Steel pp. 973–75

1. Although we generally don't think of stories as argument, they all express points of view. (In fact, everything is an argument, if we believe the title of this book.) Summarize the arguments made by each of these narratives.

Answers will vary. One possibility for the Monica Mayer narrative is that she argues for the importance of teaching

children to work hard through tough love. For Ken Kobus's narrative, the argument might be that even difficult, dangerous jobs can be beautiful and enjoyable.

2. What does each narrative teach us about work and dedication?

   Answers will vary, but the first narrative might teach us that hard physical labor is undesirable and that hard work in the academic arena will offer different rewards. The second narrative describes a great deal of beauty and happiness in the physical labor involved in steelwork.

3. In her interview, does Monica Mayer sound like a doctor as she talks? Why or why not? Is her language appropriate to the context and audience? Why or why not? Would her story have been different if she had used more formal language? Would it have been as effective? Why or why not? (For a discussion of style in arguments, see Chapter 13.)

   Answers will vary, but we think that Mayer doesn't sound much like a doctor because she uses colloquial and informal language ("half-breed," "bust my head twice up against the brick wall"). However, we also think that the tone is appropriate for a story about growing up told to a younger relative. Telling this story in more formal language would have reduced its immediacy and the feeling of what it was like for Mayer as a young girl.

4. One of Ken Kobus's arguments is that "steelmaking is just beautiful" (paragraph 3). Was such a claim surprising for you? Why? What evidence does Kobus offer? For him, what is the nature of the beauty of steelmaking? (It is, for example, not like the beauty of flowers in spring or a child's face.) In what ways is his discussion of this issue a definitional argument? (For a discussion of definitional argument, see Chapter 9.)

   Answers will vary, but one possibility is that Kobus redefines the work of steelmaking as a kind of art; his language sounds something like the description of the materials in, for example, glassblowing or sculpting. If any students are familiar with arguments about the sublime, they might argue that Kobus explains steelmaking according to those aesthetics—steelmaking as great and awe-inspiring.

5. Writing assignment

Classroom Exercise: focus on the world

Ask students to interview each other about their own work experiences and write down the narratives. What kinds of arguments are made by the students' stories of their working histories? What do we learn from the narratives that the students created?

Lisa W. Foderaro *The Well-to-Do Get Less So, and Teenagers Feel the Crunch* pp. 977–79

1. What challenges did the economic downturn present to the teenagers who are discussed in Lisa W. Foderaro's article?

   Several of the teenagers had to cut down on their discretionary spending, some had to find work, and some were unable to find work.

   In what ways were teenagers from different social classes similarly affected?

   Teenagers from different social classes had their allowances cut and so sought work.

   In what ways were the effects different? Were the differences purely quantitative (that is, different degrees of the same effects) or were they qualitative (that is, different kinds of effects)? How and why?

   Answers will vary, but we would suggest that having one's $5-per-week allowance cut is a qualitative difference from having one's allowance cut from $100 to $60 per week. From the sound of things, the young man whose $5 allowance was cut is part of a family that is in much more serious financial difficulty than the families of the teenagers who are the focus of this article; he's expected to make contributions to the family income, not just to earn money for the things he desires.

2. The article discusses the ways that high school students are expected to create a particular kind of ethos as college applicants. What consequences, if any, do you think the economic downturn might have on this application process and these expectations? Why?

Answers will vary; one possibility is that more students may apply with work experience instead of volunteer experience. In that case students may need to be more careful to explain how an entry-level job gave them important experiences as a way of building their ethos.

3. The graphic "Teenage Workers" did not appear in the print version of this article but was included in the online version. Are there aspects of the graphic that you find surprising?

   Answers will vary.

   These figures are for teens who did paid work outside the home. Work that is not paid officially (taxed by the government) is not included. Thus, work done around the house, on most farms, or in a family business was not shown on this graphic. What information does the graphic contribute to the article that is not already included in the written text?

   This graphic offers historical perspectives on teen unemployment over a few decades.

   The graph on the left, "Teens in the workforce," is discussed in some detail in the article, but the graph on the right, "Gap in unemployment rates," is not. Write a paragraph in which you describe this graphic as you would if you were using it to construct an argument of your own.

   Answers will vary.

4. Writing assignment

Classroom Exercise: focus on the world

Should teenagers be expected to work outside the home? Should low-wage, low-skilled work be considered a positive factor in a college application, or should students opt for volunteer positions? Do students who do not work develop an acceptable work ethic? If your students are traditional college-age students, they should have some authority for speaking about these questions in a roundtable discussion or class debate. If they're older, nontraditional students, they might even have stronger opinions about whether teenagers should work outside the home and what costs and benefits such work entails.

Charles Murray *Should the Obama Generation Drop Out?* pp. 982–84

Letters to the Editor *Should a College Degree Be Essential?* pp. 985–86

1. Charles Murray's argument is a proposal. Summarize the argument, paying attention to what Chapter 12 says about how to develop a proposal.

   Murray argues that employers should not require a bachelor's degree for new hires; he suggests replacing that requirement with a job-specific certification test.

   How well has Murray succeeded in developing a proposal based on the criteria that are given in that chapter? (In other words, evaluate Murray's argument as a proposal argument.)

   Answers will vary.

2. As noted, Murray is a libertarian. Libertarians place a high premium on individual liberty and the value of individuals (in contrast to the opinions of a group or society as a whole or the power of a government). Libertarians value both personal freedom and economic freedom. (This is in contrast to liberals, who place more value on personal freedom; conservatives, who place more value on economic freedom; and authoritarians or totalitarians, who value neither.) As the headnote states, Murray is from a small town in Iowa, and thanks to his intelligence (including his ability to do well on tests like the SAT), he was able to attend Harvard as an undergraduate. More recently, he has become critical of such standardized tests and the power that they have in American society. Although he once saw such tests as having a "democratizing" effect, he now contends that they no longer do so. Where do we see evidence of Murray's libertarian beliefs in this essay?

   Answers will vary. One piece of evidence for his libertarian beliefs might be his underlying premise that the most important social goal is to reduce barriers to starting work so that people can more easily choose to enter different careers. This choice potentially maximizes both personal and economic freedoms.

3. The letters to the editor that were published in response to Murray's essay demonstrate that reality is more complex than Murray

portrays it. Choose a letter that you think is especially effective in responding to Murray's proposal, and explain how it demonstrates weaknesses in his position. If none of these letters appeal to you, look on the *Times* Web site for others that were published in the *Times* in response to this article or look for substantial comments that were posted on the Web site about Murray's article. (Note that your answer to this question does not depend on your response to the essay. You may agree fully with Murray's position while still acknowledging that these letters point out aspects of the situation that he fails to address.)

Answers will vary.

4. Do you find Murray's argument convincing? Why or why not?

   Answers will vary.

   If American society were to implement Murray's proposal, what would be the consequences for colleges and universities?

   Colleges and universities might face severe budget crises if fewer students chose to pursue a bachelor's degree, but they might see a rise in the quality of their students and classes.

   For teenagers thinking about their future?

   Some teenagers would undoubtedly feel relieved that they would not have to attend college and could instead enter the workforce right away; some teenagers might be frightened by the idea that they should figure out what kind of work they want to do earlier than they thought they would need to.

   For employers?

   Some employers might struggle to develop appropriate certification tests while others might be able to come up with tests that improve their hiring efficiency.

   For society at large?

   There might be a shift in how society thinks about what constitutes authority, or how society views the value of college and university education.

   For you and your friends?

Answers will vary.

5. Writing assignment

Classroom Exercise: focus on the argument

Charles Murray's argument suggests that for some students the decision whether or not to attend college has not been much of a choice: they've always been expected to attend and they've always expected to attend, even if they weren't entirely sure why. Ask students to think carefully about what they expect from their education and what they think of what they've seen so far. Is Murray right? Are they just killing time in required classes? Ask students to write proposal arguments about what they would change about their education so far. What do they wish they were learning and experiencing, and how does that compare to what they are actually experiencing?

U.S. Bureau of Labor Statistics *Education Pays* p. 987

Laurence Shatkin *Education Pays, but Perhaps Less Than You Thought* pp. 988–90

1. According to Laurence Shatkin, why are the statistics from the U.S. Bureau of Labor Statistics at least partially misleading? (Be careful here: there is more than one step to the argument.)

   First, Shatkin notes that how much people earn is only one way of measuring their overall well-being. Second, he notes that those who earn more tend to live in places where housing costs more, thus negating some of the increases in their income.

2. What might account for the concentration of college graduates in urban areas, according to Enrico Moretti? Which hypothesis does he prefer?

   Moretti offers two hypotheses. The first is the "demand-pull hypothesis," which suggests that highly skilled workers go to cities because they are more productive there and job opportunities attract them. The second hypothesis is the "supply-pull hypothesis," which suggests that college graduates want to live in cities because they are attracted to the amenities there and that once they move there they drive rents up. Moretti prefers the demand-pull hypothesis.

The fact that Moretti does not rule out one of the two hypotheses likely means that he does not have adequate data to draw a conclusion. Do you favor one hypothesis over the other on the basis of your life experiences? Which one and why?

Answers will vary.

Why might Moretti, as an economist, not be willing to trust his life experience in answering that question?

Economists are usually trained to study and rely on inartistic proofs for their evidence, so professionally he probably values statistical trends more than personal observations.

3. Does Moretti's study or Shatkin's discussion of taxes mean that the Bureau of Labor Statistics is wrong? Why or why not?

   No, the discussion of taxes does not mean that the Bureau of Labor Statistics is wrong, because the Bureau is only reporting the median weekly earnings and not claiming to report net pay after taxes. It does, though, mean that the Bureau of Labor Statistics is only reporting partial information (but that's often true of a statistical report).

4. Chapter 4 discusses statistics as examples of hard evidence or what Aristotle termed "inartistic appeals." What does this selection remind us about the nature and limitations of so-called hard evidence?

   Hard evidence can still leave out some information; for example, in this article the fact that those with more education make more money does not address issues such as how far that money goes, how it contributes to quality of life, and so on.

5. Writing assignment

Classroom Exercise: focus on the argument

The results of the research discussed in this reading might trouble some students, especially those who have taken out significant loans to finance their education. What is their education worth to them? What amount would they not pay to attend college? What kind of return do they expect on their investment in economic terms? What about in non-economic measures? What kinds of rewards and benefits do they expect will accompay their college education experience?

Sandy Baum and Jennifer Ma for the College Board *Education Pays: The Benefits of Higher Education for Individuals and Society* pp. 991–1006

1. What goals did the College Board have in producing this report?

   The main goals were to provide evidence for the benefits and importance of higher education, which might also be a way of arguing for the College Board's importance.

   What goals do Sandy Baum and Jennifer Ma state that it did *not* have? (See, for example, paragraph 21.)

   They do not intend to analyze the causes or offer solutions for the differences in postsecondary education among different groups.

   How does this report help the College Board realize its goals?

   This report offers a great deal of evidence, especially in the form of inartistic proofs, about the effects of a college education.

   In what ways does the report represent an argument of fact? (For a discussion of arguments of fact, see Chapter 8.)

   The report first describes a situation that leads to questions about the facts of that situation (whether higher education is worth it for individuals and for society), makes a claim that higher education is indeed valuable, and then offers substantial evidence supporting that claim.

2. Who is the intended audience for the report? (Assume that there are several intended audiences. Who might they be, and why?)

   Answers will vary, but press students to explain their answers. One likely audience is higher education administrators, who might publicize a report such as this with legislators or others who control funding for higher education organizations.

3. Paragraphs 14–17 discuss the challenges of understanding and using statistical information. How does this discussion contribute to the ethos of the College Board, as publisher of the report?

   Answers will vary, but by pointing out possible ways that the data could be misread and explaining that the data might also leave out important information, the College

Board probably enhances their ethos. Readers are likely to see them as fair-minded and confident enough in their claim to be aware of the limitations of and possible rebuttals to their argument.

How does it seek to prevent the misuse of the data included in this report? (A correlation is a relationship between two phenomena that, as noted, cannot be interpreted as one of cause and effect. For example, skin cancer rates are high among tennis players in the Southwest. Thus, there is a correlation between frequently playing tennis in the Southwest and developing skin cancer. But playing tennis itself doesn't cause skin cancer anywhere, including the Southwest, so there is no cause-and-effect relationship between tennis and cancer. The high level of skin cancer there is linked to high levels of sun exposure.)

Most of all, the report tries to warn against interpreting correlation as causation so that readers of the report will understand that the effects of a college education may not be entirely clear.

4. What is your response to this excerpt? How aware were you of the information presented here? Does this information encourage you to think in new ways about your efforts to get a college education? Why or why not? If so, how?

   Answers will vary.

5–6. Writing assignments

Classroom Exercise: focus on the world

It's unlikely that any current college student sat down to read a report like this before deciding to pursue higher education. So what did cause the students to attend? What influences played a part in their decision to attend the particular school they now attend? Ask students to write down as many causes as they can remember; then spend some time discussing what constituted authority and good evidence as they made their decision about college.

Alesia Montgomery *Kitchen Conferences and Garage Cubicles: The Merger of Home and Work in the 24–7 Global Economy* pp. 1008–22

1. The opening paragraph of this study explains that Alesia Montgomery is interested in the "mergers of paid work and family life." Rather than relying on questionnaires, surveys, or even interviews alone, she uses ethnography—prolonged participant observation where the researcher in some sense becomes part of the lives of those studied. What kinds of evidence might such observation yield? What benefits might there be to studying a specific case in detail? What limitations?

   Such close observation could potentially offer evidence that the subjects might wish to cover up or that they might not realize is important or that they did not realize was even evidence. Studying a specific case in detail means that the researcher will have great depth of knowledge about this case and will understand particular details and nuances very well. However, the researcher might also see an outlier or atypical example that he or she comes to think of as normal, or might not be able to see patterns that would become apparent from studying more cases through interviews or surveys.

2. How does the review of earlier studies about the gendered nature of work and family life provide necessary background for this study? How does it create a context for this study? Was this information new to you?

   The review of earlier studies establishes why the study of the modern arrangement works by placing Marjaneh's practices in a historical framework.

3. One of Montgomery's concerns is how technological advances are shaping contemporary life. How is this concern manifested in her report of Marjaneh and Steve's life?

   Montgomery carefully explains how Marjaneh and Steve negotiate the technology in their lives; the best example might be the extended explanation of how Marjaneh must struggle to find appropriate settings in which to place and receive phone calls.

   In what ways is this topic an organizing principle of her discussion?

   Because the spaces in the house are, to some degree, defined by the technology in them, technological advances contribute to the organization of the report.

4. Ethnographers are generally concerned with issues of space and the ways that the use of space shapes human interaction. How do we see this concern reflected in Montgomery's analysis?

   Montgomery includes significant descriptions of how the family does different kinds of work in different rooms in the house.

   What role does the figure on p. 1014 play in Montgomery's description and analysis? Why is it important to her argument?

   The figure helps her readers to understand the physical space that she describes the family operating in, and the diagram of the house is much easier to understand than a written description would be.

5. On first reading an ethnographic study, students who are not familiar with the genre sometimes claim that no data are presented. How might Montgomery respond? In other words, for an ethnographer, what counts as data?

   Ethnographers rely on observations and descriptions, so Montgomery's account of what she observed is her data.

6. Writing assignment

Classroom Exercise: focus on the world

In what ways does the space on campus or at home shape students' lives? Beginning with a discussion of classroom arrangement, ask students to analyze how a particular space helps shape their experience. For example, they might examine their workspace, assuming one exists, in their current home to see how it does and does not contribute to efficient working. But you might also take students outside the classroom to different parts of campus to have them observe how people interact in different physical spaces. How does the configuration of walkways or furniture affect people? You might even have students write mini-ethnographies focused on the space that they experience in their daily lives.

Stewart D. Friedman	*The Fallacy of "Work-Life Balance"*	pp. 1024–25
	Take the Four-Way View	pp. 1026–38

1. What argument is Stewart D. Friedman making in the video that is excerpted on the Amazon.com Web site? In what ways is it a defi-

nitional argument? (In addition to the features of definition argument discussed in Chapter 9, note that a common strategy in a definitional argument is saying what something is *not*, as Friedman does here.)

Friedman argues that "balance" is the wrong metaphor for figuring out how to live our lives. By rejecting the metaphor of balance, Friedman attempts to redefine how we think about our lives.

How is ethos created in this short video? (Consider not only what is said but also how it is packaged.)

First, the logo for Harvard Business Publishing, which opens the video and stays in the corner throughout the presentation, associates the author with a prestigious academic institution. Second, his suit and the formal background create an air of seriousness. Third, his academic tone and the precision of his speech help establish a sense of expertise.

2. Focus on the structure of the chapter from *Total Leadership*. (You may wish to list the titles of the sections and exercises in the order in which they occur to help you analyze the chapter's structure.) To what extent and in what ways is this chapter organized according to the principles of stasis theory (which are discussed in Chapter 1) or the categories of argument that are presented in the text (arguments of fact, arguments of definition, arguments of evaluation, causal arguments, and proposals)?

   Friedman opens the chapter by referring to the previous chapter, which asked readers to recognize the fact of the four domains. In the next section he instructs readers to define the domains. After that, he asks readers to evaluate how their attention to different domains fits their values and to investigate why (causes) their lives are ordered as they are now. The end of the chapter could be read as a proposal argument for reshaping one's life according to the values clarified by the exercise.

   Why is such an organization appropriate, given Friedman's goals?

   Friedman wants to move his readers through a process and to propose to readers a new way of imagining their lives, so

he needs to move them through the steps of stasis theory to establish the problem and find a solution for it.

3. How does Friedman use the extended examples of Victor and Roxanne to advance his argument?

   We might think of them as emotional arguments: reading about how actual people experience the steps that Friedman recommends allows us to connect the goals of the program with our own lives as we recognize similar struggles to allocate our time and energy.

   Would his argument be less effective without these examples? Why? What specific roles do they play in the argument?

   Answers will vary, though we suggest that without the examples the argument would feel too abstract.

4. What role do the activities in the chapter play in Friedman's argument?

   The activities encourage readers to participate in the reading and to develop their own arguments about what's happening in their own lives.

   What did you learn from doing them, for example? (If you didn't complete them, do so now.)

   Answers will vary.

   How are these activities indicated in the text?

   They are set off with a different typography and a box that marks them as separate from the rest of the text.

   How effective is the layout of the text in this regard?

   Answers will vary.

   What roles do Figures 3–1 and 3–2 play in Friedman's argument? What are the benefits of including two figures, rather than simply relying on one?

   These figures help readers see how to create their own responses, and the differences between them help readers understand that there's not only one way to graph this information.

5. Writing assignment

Classroom Exercise: focus on the argument

Friedman argues that the metaphor of balance is not a good one for thinking about our lives. Have students brainstorm other metaphors for their lives. For example, some critics say that Homer's epic poems, the *Iliad* and the *Odyssey*, set out two primary metaphors for our lives, life as a battle and life as a journey. What other metaphors can students come up with to describe their lives? Ask them to write a definition argument in which they defend a particular metaphor as being especially useful for thinking about their lives.

Wrap-up Exercises for "What Are You Working For?"

1. What does your ideal work life look like? How does it balance work and leisure, what sorts of rewards (not just financial) does it offer, and what kind of preparation does it require? For this evaluative argument, be sure that you use the tools provided by Toulmin logic—carefully defend your claim with adequate evidence, warrants, and backing.
2. What does work teach? What should we learn from working? What *do* we learn from working—is it always positive? That is, can some kinds of work teach lessons that we might regret learning? Based on your own experience and/or the experiences of those you know and interview, write an essay that takes a position on the lessons afforded by work, however you wish to define it.
3. Using the evidence provided by the readings in this chapter, write an essay in which you make a claim for how your school should prepare students for their working lives. Should your school teach students how to think about how work fits into the rest of one's life, as Stewart Friedman does? Should your school prepare workers for a world where their home and work lives will intersect seamlessly? Should your school not worry about preparing people for work at all but instead focus on a broad education that emphasizes skills and thinking?